A THOUSAND SHARDS OF GLASS

A THOUSAND SHARDS OF GLASS

There is Another America

Michael Katakis

SCRIBNER

LONDON NEW YORK SYDNEY TORONTO NEW DELHI

First published in Great Britain by Simon & Schuster UK Ltd, 2014
This paperback edition published by Scribner, an imprint of Simon & Schuster UK Ltd, 2020
A CBS COMPANY

SCRIBNER and design are registered trademarks of The Gale Group, Inc.,
used under licence by Simon & Schuster Inc.

10 9 8 7 6 5 4 3 2 1

Simon & Schuster UK Ltd
1st Floor
222 Gray's Inn Road
London WC1X 8HB

Simon & Schuster Australia, Sydney
Simon & Schuster India, New Delhi

www.simonandschuster.co.uk
www.simonandschuster.com.au
www.simonandschuster.co.in

A CIP catalogue record for this book
is available from the British Library

Paperback ISBN: 978-1-4711-8919-7
eBook ISBN: 978-1-4711-3145-5

Typeset in Bell by M Rules
Printed and bound by CPI Group (UK) Ltd, Croydon CR0 4YY

For Kris

I've kept a lock of your
Hair and some of your dust
As a talisman, protection
From the memories, like a
Siren's songs that deceive and
Rust

You were my True North
My bearings, my home, but
Death, envious of our course
Folded you into his silence
Setting me adrift without she
Who was my map, my love

I bring what you are with me,
To London and Rome, to the
Greek lemon hills you loved and
Into the Ligurian Sea where once,
Amid the Dancing Stars, we bathed

You are everywhere, my silent
Traveling companion

and for
Mrs. Mary Katharine Lewis,
my Charlotte Shaw

CONTENTS

PREFACE TO THE 2020 EDITION:
AMERICA'S MYTH OF GOODNESS

> Our progress in degeneracy appears to me to be pretty rapid. As a nation, we begin by declaring that, 'all men are created equal'. We now practically read it, 'all men are created equal, except negroes'. When the Know-Nothings get control, it will read, 'all men are created equal, except negroes, and foreigners, and Catholics'. When it comes to this I should prefer emigrating to some country where they make no pretense of loving liberty – to Russia, for instance, where despotism can be taken pure, and without the base alloy of hypocrisy.

> Abraham Lincoln in a letter to Joshua F. Speed about the anti-immigrant 'Know Nothing Party' of the 1850s.

People and nations are propelled and held back by their myths. Myth is repeated over time, generation after generation, until it evolves into a narrative that promotes a constructed good while deleting a nation's darker truths.

Myth is a long-term advertising campaign that sells a fiction that when successfully absorbed 'is' true. And yet, the shadows of what has been nag at the national conscience like an unwelcomed stranger at our collective doors. The history of real intentions and deeds are not so easily erased.

A belief in such myths is a kind of sleepwalking that does not require thought. In fact, myth is preferable for anyone who does not wish to think at all. You don't even need to write your own words or opinions. One need only parrot the tired slogans of, 'Make America Great Again' or, 'America is the greatest nation on earth' or, '... all men are created equal'. Repeating them succeeds in drowning out, for a time, a more complete history, allowing perpetrators and the ignorant an escape hatch from the truth; but, just like the Wizard of Oz, the illusion only works if you don't look behind the curtain.

My country, the United States, has been drowning in myth for a long time. We have myths about our courage and equality, our piousness and how god is on our side. There is the myth about our kindness, generosity and inclusiveness and how much we care about children and each other. There are myths about our sense of justice and how we want to make the world safe for Democracy and how our capitalistic system is the greatest engine for creating prosperity. In short, we Americans have an overinflated myth about our goodness that, in spite of much evidence to the contrary, we pass on to the world, and ourselves, as true. However, one need only peek behind the curtain to see what is really going on, and what is going on is very troubling indeed because the lies we tell ourselves have a very high cost. It is a cost that is bankrupting our humanity and, brick by brick, dismantling ideas and institutions that we had once hoped would speak to more than ledgers recording profit and loss.

Millions of Americans have become small people who are afraid of their own shadows. They have sacrificed truth and reason for carnival barkers offering empty and ugly promises. In such a society, it is nearly impossible to entertain, let alone inculcate, morality and ethics into daily lives and actions. We have been here before but most Americans don't know that because, as Gore Vidal wrote, 'Americans know nothing because they remember nothing.'

One of America's claims to goodness is that we love our children. Notice I say 'our' children because, at the time of this writing, President Donald Trump and his minions are separating children from their parents. The majority of these people have crossed the American border illegally hoping to find some relief from the terrible violence they are running from. To those in power, it does not make a difference if the people are seeking asylum from gangs, failed countries or domestic and societal abuse. Thousands of children who are already traumatized by war and violence come to a country that they hope will be kind and empathetic, where they might find a moment's peace, only to be traumatized further when they are separated from their parents by uniformed officers who say, 'I'm just following orders.' Where have we heard that one before?

Agreed: People should not come into a country illegally. However, we must never become monsters when carrying out the law.

For many Americans, when it comes to other people's children, no matter what they tell themselves, the truth is that millions of them don't give a damn. For children in far away places, trying to escape tyranny and violence – too often with the finger prints of the United States, Russia, Britain and France on them – 'care' is often set aside when confronted with a manufactured threat or corporate business interests. It is millions of Americans as they have always been and it is who we are still. To be sure, not everyone, but millions of so-called 'good' people.

In America, we feel that by saying how much we care, we have done something virtuous, not unlike the confessional where one is forgiven their trespasses with a few Hail Mary's. Once absolved, the admitted sinner is free to go on their merry way and do it again. It's a great racket but one with a high, hidden cost.

In America, our claim that we care about our children, let alone other people's children, is put into question based upon not alternative truths but facts.

The 2014 National Vital Statistics Report shows that in 2010 the US ranked twenty-sixth among twenty-nine OECD countries with regard to infant death. When compared to all wealthy industrialized nations, the United States ranks last or nearly last, year after year. Those 'facts' would suggest that the myth of how much we love our own children is questionable at best and further questions why, in what is supposedly the greatest and richest nation on earth, does the US stay at the bottom of lists regarding infant mortality when compared to every other western industrialized nation? A nation's myth of goodness is a powerful tool that assists people in turning away from the realities that surround them, at least for a time.

During the lead up to the invasion of Iraq, lapel-pin patriots in the George W. Bush administration put out many untruths, and did so under the guise of objectivity and love of country. Planning to go to war for their own interests and agendas, the Bush administration used any information, no matter how questionable, to make a case for the invasion they were determined to execute no matter the evidence to the contrary. It was, as one Bush administration official put it, an advertising campaign to the American public.

The sale was a success but no advertising campaign could save the once cheering people from the realities of the lies and the tragic and dismal failures that followed. Now, many years later, those actions that did not entertain doubt continue to exact a cost in lives and treasure with no end in sight.

What is striking is that millions of Americans do not know about their own country's history and what we have been doing for a long time. Prior to the invasion of Iraq, many people – mostly liberals – were appalled at the thought that we might invade a country preemptively. They behaved as if the United States had not done such things before and claimed such actions did not reflect American values or 'who we were'. The conduct of millions of Americans, including liberals, during the lead up to the invasion of Iraq, was that of blind patriotism. It was understandable, to a point, but in the end, as Voltaire wrote, 'anyone who can make you believe in absurdities can make you commit atrocities.'

Americans, shocked by the attacks of September 11, chose not to look behind the curtain. If they had, they would have seen the scoundrels who were selling a war, based upon America's myth of goodness, with fear and lies. They are the people George Orwell would have recognized, people like Dick Cheney or Henry Kissinger or Donald Trump: the kind who promote then profit from war, but are 'the kind of person who is far away when the trigger is pulled'.

Americans of many stripes turned away when they knew enhanced interrogation was torture. Choosing to rationalize actions that our enemies used and were deemed against international law, we, the United States, like some con man on the street, used sleight of hand to create the illusion that we were on the up and up. But we knew exactly what we were doing. It is not surprising then that the United States is not a signatory to the International Criminal Court.

So much for our myth about the rule of law.

When the country desperately needed Americans to stand and say no to the criminality being done in their name, millions remained seated.

Some liberal politicians argued that the nation invading Iraq was not the 'real' America that they knew to be just and good.

I found all the carrying-on amusing and sad, and was reminded again of Gore Vidal, who said about himself and America:

> Whenever I want to know what my country is up to, I look into my own black heart.

The idea that the invasion of Iraq was something new for America was laughable to those who knew anything about the history of the United States. Some people suggested that the invasion of Iraq was about oil. Many administration officials came forward, as did others in the media, to say that it was for humanitarian and security reasons. Many people believed the twaddle, including some pretty intelligent ones like Christopher Hitchens, but anyone who knew America's 'black heart' understood that 'humanitarian reasons' or 'freeing the Iraqi people' was the last thing on America's mind.

In *Overthrow: America's Century of Regime Change From Hawaii to Iraq*, Stephen Kinzer details that what the United States did in Iraq was nothing new. Kinzer writes:

> The invasion of Iraq in 2003 was not an isolated episode. It was the culmination of a 110-year period during which Americans overthrew fourteen governments that displeased them for various ideological, political and economic reasons. Like each of these operations, the 'regime change' in Iraq seemed for a time – a very short time – to have worked. It is now clear, however, that this operation has had terrible unintended consequences. So have most of the

other coups, revolutions and invasions that the United States has mounted to depose governments it feared or mistrusted.

So much for learning from our mistakes.

When America elected its first black president there was hope that the country had turned a historic corner. But it was only to find that the nation's 'original sin' came bubbling up from the dark holes where it had always been.

There was a Southern congressman who yelled, 'You lie' during the president's State of the Union speech and claimed that the president was not a real American because he had not been born in the United States. Even when it was shown beyond any doubt, the current president of the United States, Donald Trump, continued to publicly promote doubt, racism and hatred in the body politic with millions of Americans not caring if it was true. As one Trump supporter in London told me after I had asked, 'What if everything the president says is a lie?', the man responded by saying, 'I don't care if he's lying. He's saying what I want to hear.' I know, dear reader, it's hard to get your head around that one.

Many Republican leaders have fomented division and conspiracy theories for a long time and their followers have been complicit with the lies because it served their purposes, at least for a while. When President Obama was elected, Republicans wasted little time declaring it their mission to make sure that the new president failed.

So much for the myth of patriotism and love of country.

For a long time Democrats talked down to people and then they morphed into something arrogant and silly. What the party had become, starting with Clinton, bore no resemblance to the Democrats I remember as a kid in Chicago, who represented factory workers and plumbers and all the folks who didn't play golf on the weekends or sip Chardonnay.

The Democrats abandoned who they were and what they stood for, and forgot that there was a difference between making money and earning it. They became Republican-lite, created NAFTA and gave corporations more power over people's lives with policies that helped ship jobs overseas, where corporations could exploit people who had no redress. Nothing is as profitable for corporations as a workforce that can't object.

Democrats, through their own myths, thought they were for the working and middle classes but in reality they betrayed the working man while Republicans, since Reagan, never gave a damn about them in the first place. But who are all these Republicans and Democrats? They are us. I think it always wise to remember that self-serving con men and women of any persuasion only care about two things: what you can do for them and what you can do to them.

After all is said and done, it is finally the citizen who is responsible. I grew up in the Midwest and I remember the dreadful racist talk that was considered normal. Then I lived in Philadelphia and it was worse. As I traveled the country, negative attitudes toward race were always there in one form or another.

Americans themselves have sold out their neighbors and communities by abandoning their main streets, instead choosing to shop at the Walmarts and Targets filled with cheap Chinese products. Those choices have had devastating outcomes with ever more jobs lost. It was not just government and corporations that reduced the country to a nickel-and-dime store and the people into harvestable crops. Many people had a hand in selling-out their own neighbors and country for a perceived bargain.

So much for 'we are all in this together'

Americans' actions and votes have, in part, brought us to where we are today. It is the result of short-term thinking or no thinking at all. In these United States of Salesmen we have shown each other and the world, time and again, who so many of us are. It seems understandable then, that millions of us would vote for a grifter selling snake oil, to be president of the United States. He's just like us. He is millions of 'us'.

In 2014, when I wrote *A Thousand Shards of Glass*, my dear wife Kris was dying from a brain tumor. What I had to say about America was tough but true. Today, in 2019, it is much worse.

In 2014, I was profoundly angry at the American medical system for how it treated my wife, whom insurance companies and others called a customer. My fellow Americans, by their lack of empathy and insatiable greed, stole the remaining time I had left with my dying wife. After nearly seven years I still have not found a way to forgive them.

While the anger from that time has softened, I find it is

returning because millions of Americans are again showing the cruel face of who they are without pause or shame, by following a president who brings out the worst in Americans' black hearts.

As a boy, I was taught that I would be judged by the company I kept. I have chosen not to join the millions of Americans who now stand with President Trump, the Ku Klux Klan, the American Nazi party and other abhorrent groups and individuals who make up the nation's 'dark side'.

Many of my fellow Americans have made a choice to remain seated while cruel and illegal acts are perpetrated in their names. Perhaps one day they will come to regret that when the times called for courage and decency, they remained silent and, by their silence, became collaborators in one of the nation's darkest hours.

INTRODUCTION:
A THOUSAND SHARDS OF GLASS

> This land of such dear souls, this dear dear land,
> Dear for her reputation through the world,
> Is now leas'd out – I die pronouncing it –
> Like to a tenement or pelting farm.
> England, bound in with the triumphant sea,
> Whose rocky shore beats back the envious siege
> Of wat'ry Neptune, is now bound in with shame,
> With inky blots and rotten parchment bonds;
> That England, that was wont to conquer others,
> Hath made a shameful conquest of itself.
>
> Shakespeare, *Richard II*, II, i

There is another America and it lies just beneath the surface of myth, adrift on a sea of illusions and imprisoned by implacable ideologies that strangle reason and compassion. We are not in this together.

The real America is a place obsessed with religion but not ethics, with law, not justice. It is neither the democracy nor the capitalist society touted by corporations, politicians and the media, who perform their own kabuki dance of pretend objectivity when in reality they're another cog in the corporate state, dependent on its largesse. What is most disturbing, however, is the willful indifference and arrogance that has now made many Americans comfortable with injustice, both at home and abroad.

In the 'United States of Salesmen' it matters little what is in one's heart. It is the verbal, animated gestures of patriotism and faith, no matter how insincere, which are the measure of one's 'Americaness' today. Straighten your stars and stripes lapel-pin, adjust your tie and, no matter what you see and hear, just remain seated. Forgive me but I prefer to stand and I have never much cared for 'club' pins on my clothing.

America's capacity for self-delusion is equaled only by its hypocrisy, which for decades has allowed us, without a hint of irony, to lecture other nations on human rights while torturing people in our custody. America has long spoken of democratic values while working tirelessly during the twentieth century and before to thwart democratic movements and elected governments that have not coincided with our national interests, which has often meant nothing more than forcible corporate access to other people's property. General Smedley Butler, one of America's most decorated soldiers, who, I assume, was exhausted by the hypocrisy himself, wrote in his 1935 book *War is a Racket*: 'I spent 33 years [in the Marines] ... most of my time being a high class muscle man for Big Business, for Wall Street and the bankers. In short, I was a racketeer ... for capitalism.'

A great many Americans have never fully understood that the past does not reside in some dead history. It is always being retold, passed between sister and brother, from parent to child, creating new resentments about unaccounted for transgressions. Those histories roll in front of us until we run into them again like an unresolved Freudian dream. Far from being something to be avoided in the future, however, in America this repetition of manufactured and unresolved conflict is for some their bread and butter, or as the gangsters in the movies say just before they shoot their fellow Mafioso, 'This is nothing personal. It's just business.' And business is exactly what it is.

We are not who we think we are or, more accurately, we are not who we sell ourselves as. America is a nationalistic state filled with 'actor patriots' such as the now deified Ronald Reagan who, along with others like George W. Bush and the draft-averse Dick Cheney, represent the so-called 'modern Republican Party' which, by the way, eerily resembles the Mississippi Democratic Party of the 1950s, with all the trimmings such as voter disenfranchisement, shameless bigotry and corruption, and is filled with the type of patriot George Orwell once described as 'the kind of person who is somewhere else when the trigger is pulled'. In such a patriotic country it seems rather odd that less than 1 per cent of the population would serve.

Our patriotism is all performance of course, bread and circus designed at once to divide and mollify an ever undereducated middle and lower class whose attention span and empathy for others seem to decrease with each new Apple product that is released. For over a half century, America has been a store disguised as a country. As a people we have scarcely moved beyond de Tocqueville's early description of Americans: 'The majority lives in the perpetual utterance of self-applause, and there are certain truths which the Americans can learn only from strangers or from experience'. The self-imposed lack of civic evolution has made for model consumers but poor citizens.

I have read some criticisms over the years asserting that the United States has become just a bunch of second-rate salesmen. I beg to differ. The salesmen and women in these United States of Salesmen are astounding. They have refined deceit and trickery to such an art that they are able to convince a large swath of the middle class that it is in their interests to oppose National Health Insurance and instead put their fate, and those of their loved ones, in the hands of health insurance companies who have a 'pre-existing' interest in denying coverage once it is sold. These brilliant sales people can even sell additional war to an already economically and, dare I say, spiritually broken nation.

These magnificent hucksters have convinced desperate people that 'for profit' universities, which of course are not universities at all, are their best bet to achieve the 'American Dream' that always seems just a bit out of reach these days. Once sold, these good people, trying to better themselves, take out guaranteed government student loans to pay the high tuition fees of the so-called universities, thinking that they are on their way to a better tomorrow. At the end of their

Oz journey the optimistic graduates leave the glittering malls of learning with nothing more than a piece of paper and a mountain of debt. The desperate are often left more desperate and broken than ever.

These artists of deceit have found a way to preach 'privatization' and 'the free market' while bilking the student and the taxpayer at the same time. But really they are not so clever. They are just allowed to run roughshod because a percentage of the public money they receive gets recycled back into the political parties, and then, with the compliance of their paid senators, congressmen and congressional staffs, they all work together to weaken the protections that the salesmen find obstructive to their hustle. These are the best crooks around and they are in the business of arms, drugs, communications and banking and in a medical business that is even more rapacious and savage than what I witnessed as a boy in Chicago.

The salesmen I speak of are not benign: far from it. They have long been the soft terrorists among us, the ones who whisper into the ears of politicians and generals, telling them that it is in the country's interest to invade Chile or back Diem, or kill him. They are the invisible hands that push the computer keys denying a woman with cancer her treatment when they know her claim is valid. They do not wish to tell you what is in your food or water or where the ingredients in the formula that you are feeding your baby come from. They are about secrecy and monopoly and are profoundly undemocratic.

I assume that some of you are bristling at the words

already written and I can hear some of you repeating the overused American mantra, 'Why do you have to be so negative?' or, the current conversation stopper, 'Why do you hate America?' In answer to such questions, I would simply state first, that it is not I who is negative but the evidence itself, and secondly, I do not hate America but I am profoundly disappointed and ashamed of the United States and the American people.

To the more sensitive reader who is saying about now, 'But surely there are good, decent and enlightened people in the United States, right?' I would agree, but they are not in charge and they are a minority and it is essential, if we are to evolve, that we first tell the truth about ourselves to each other. Like Caesar's own 'point of no return' we too have crossed the Rubicon, with the tragic consequences of endowing the most corrupt among us power over the essentials of our lives.

No, we are not in this together, but we should be, for John Donne was right: we are all part of the main, whether we know it or not, and the bell finally does toll for thee. Personally, I think it is better to stand together and care for one another than to be a thousand shards of glass that cut and scar for nothing more than a handful of silver.

1   DYING THE AMERICAN WAY

To the living we owe respect,
but to the dead we owe only the truth.

Voltaire

At the time of this writing, in the next room, my dear wife is
dying. It is only a matter of hours, I have been told, until the
brain tumor that has tried to take her for over five years will
finally end her existence and its own, in a rather odd victory.

The beginning of our family ordeal arrived with a whisper.
First came the soft, terrifying voices and later the auditory
hallucinations that my wife worried might be the first signs
of madness. After being assured that was not the case, she
found that the hallucinations lessened, only to be followed by
a persistent headache that intensified each day.

On a sunny California morning she rose and said that the
headache had worsened and then said, 'You don't think I have
a brain tumor, do you?'

Seeing the concern in her eyes I immediately hugged her
and said, 'Oh sweetie, no. It's probably those allergies of yours

acting up again,' not for a moment thinking that such a horrible thing could be true, for Kris and I still lived on that side of the river where the illusion of past well-being lulls one into a sense of present security. It is finally illness that wakes us from such dreams and in a moment we find ourselves on the opposite bank looking back to see who we once were.

'I think we should go to the hospital,' she said.

So began our descent into the bowels of a brutal and savage corporate medical business, one that would prove nearly as traumatic as the tumor itself. For in America, from the beginning, my wife, as with millions of others, was not looked upon as a patient but rather as a consumer, which meant being seen as an opportunity by some and a liability by others.

In all my travels throughout the world, I have never heard of terminal patients being referred to as customers except in the United States, and that alone speaks volumes about who we are and what we value. It is no wonder then that, from the beginning of Kris' illness, patients, doctors and nurses told me that in America a patient must have an advocate. How strange.

The (second) definition of advocate in the *Oxford English Dictionary* is 'a person who pleads a case on someone else's behalf'. The word 'pleads' is quite appropriate in our case, for I have had to plead and threaten, trick and yell and cry and yell again and write endless letters and threaten with violence to get what I needed for my wife's care. And we are the supposed 'lucky ones' with insurance.

One can quickly see why someone thrust into such savagery at such a vulnerable time needs an advocate. But why is the system, and let's be frank, the system is 'us', in such a state? The reason is quite simple: it's the money. No ethics apply, for the idea of ethics is but a quaint afterthought in the United States, something that is said in order to allow people to live with themselves and avoid seeing the monsters they have become. Yes, monsters do exist.

The American medical business is best described as a giant machine with a million moving parts. Each one of those million parts is owned by a different entity, most of whom do not communicate with the other because they are in competition and thus adversarial. It becomes apparent very quickly, once someone is trapped within the system, that all of the talk of 'service' and 'choice' is a constructed fiction for the protection of corporate interests and the promotion of a 'product' which is, at its heart, the illusion of security. The promises made prior to an illness quickly evaporate at the most desperate of times to reveal a labyrinth of conditions, ever-changing rules and small print that not only fails to soothe or elucidate but terrifies instead.

Contained within this machine is an endless Kafka-like nightmare that buries the ill and their families in sheets of paper that no one can understand, resulting in endless calls from strangers demanding more and more money. The faceless people manning the machine reach out their never satiated hands to unendingly ask the ill and dying for more of everything. In this, the United States is unique when compared to any other western industrialized nation.

When a woman from the hospital's business office called to tell me that I owed the hospital more money, I reminded her that a doctor at the hospital had made arrangements for my wife and I not to be bothered again concerning fees. 'And I wish that the doctor had never helped you and your wife with those arrangements,' she said.

I suspect she thought us unworthy of any consideration since I'd questioned so many indecipherable bills, or perhaps it was my audacity at going over her head and expecting that my wife would be treated with empathy and courtesy. During the five years I was dealing with such people, it always felt as though I were in a den of jackals that saw my wife as nothing more than a line item in their budget. Their callousness and indifference filled me with fear, leaving me to think that I needed to be ever vigilant so as to protect my wife from their intrusions and demands while she fought for her life.

The disease that struck down Kris was no one's fault but the dreadful behavior that followed was. This is my opinion of course, but an informed one based upon many unpleasant experiences that never seemed to end and which increasingly robbed my wife and me of the time we had left together. I have often wondered if any of those people ever thought that such abhorrent conduct might put murder in people's hearts. It did in mine.

The machine is also unjust to the point of farce. After not being able to get a claim settled as Mr. Michael Katakis over a five-month period, I resorted to using my appointed title of 'Ambassador' and spoke to a supervisor from our insurance company, who settled the claim in less than forty minutes. I asked him if he thought it appropriate that as Mr. Katakis I could get nothing done but as Ambassador the claim was settled in a matter of minutes.

'No, it is not appropriate,' he answered.

'What about others who are sick but have no advocate, or are not so persistent, or are not ambassadors?' I asked, and was met with a silence that thankfully seemed a bit like shame.

The machine is also incompetent. When my wife received calls from the hospice nurses asking if they should come, Kris would assess how she felt and sometimes tell me, 'You know, I am feeling fairly well today. Let's not burden the nurse. She's already spread very thin and this will give her a chance to spend more time with someone who really needs her today.'

Kris did that often. She is a kind and considerate human being but the machine does not reward such behavior. When the time came that Kris and I did need hospice respite, she was declined. Terminal tumor aside, the machine had decided that because Kris had been coping without hospice care for so long, she was not sufficiently unwell to need it now. This suggested to us that going forward we should use all resources available to us, even when not needed, so as not to be denied other services that were. Such is the efficiency and wisdom of the private American medical business.

When the insurance executive was called again by me, the Ambassador, the problem was rectified within thirty minutes but by then, after a week had already passed, Kris was too ill to be moved.

Then, there was the nameless woman who called and asked for Kris only days after she had returned home from her first brain surgery in 2007.

'This is the [hospital] billing department. May I speak to Kris Hardin?'

'Kris cannot come to the phone. I'm her husband. May I help you?'

'Yes, you have an outstanding bill of twelve hundred dollars. When might we receive payment?'

'As you might imagine things are rather difficult here at present after Kris' surgery and diagnosis. I have just received something from the insurance company saying it has paid seventy-five thousand dollars, with I think another eighty thousand pending. I don't have the paper right here.'

'Yes, but you are not covered for doctors' fees.'

'What are you talking about? My wife was told that we were completely covered.'

'Well, you are completely covered here, but not for doctors' fees. The doctors here do not accept payment from your insurance company.'

'But that means we are not fully covered. That is not what we were told by a doctor at the hospital. Are you saying that we are covered and not covered at the same time?'

'Well, I'm sorry, but you were misinformed. Now the bill is twelve hundred dollars and how would you like to pay?'

'Yes, we were misinformed and you have misinformed me again. You said that we are covered and then you say "except for …". But if there is an exception then you cannot say we are "fully" covered. Also, we were misinformed by one of your doctors and it would seem it was done to keep my wife in your hospital. I am going to have to check things out before I pay anything because now I'm worried and confused. Are you saying that all doctors' fees concerning my wife's treatment will not be covered?'

'Yes, they will not be covered.'

'But that means another ten or twenty thousand dollars, right? I need to find that somewhere. The hospital at the University of California, San Francisco takes our insurance, so why don't you? And why would a doctor misrepresent the facts and not advise that we go to what is one of the best brain tumor facilities in the country, which I have just learned is UCSF?'

'We are not UCSF and perhaps your wife just misunder-stood.'

'Well, Madam, I have not had brain surgery and I can barely understand you now. When calling in the future, please ask for me. My wife is in no condition to speak to you and I do not want her upset or worried. It won't help her recovery.'

'I will make a note, but you will need to pay this bill.'

'Not until I get to the bottom of this.'

'Please be advised then that if payment is not received within the time it is due it may be referred to collections.'

'Ma'am, I have already told you what I intend to do.'

Some days later the business office called again and asked to speak to Kris Hardin. Once again I told them that Kris was not to be disturbed. They must not ask for her. I continued, detailing how we had been billed for mental health in Bakersfield,

California. I told the woman that we had never been to Bakersfield nor had Kris received any mental health assistance from anyone, anywhere and I was not prepared to pay any bill until I understood it. The woman began to negotiate with me.

'Okay, you don't owe twelve hundred dollars, you owe eight hundred and fifty. How's that?'

'Eight hundred and fifty dollars for what? In the last conversation I had with someone from your office I stated that we had never been told about doctors' fees, had been misinformed about being completely covered by a doctor at the hospital, that I was going to get to the bottom of the issue, but that my first responsibility at present was to my wife's care. I also said that my wife was not to be contacted and here you are asking to speak to her days later. Do you understand that she has just undergone brain surgery for brain cancer and can't even do basic math at present? What is wrong with you?'

'I'm so sorry and yes, I will make a note, but you will have to take care of this balance.'

One day, unknown to me, Kris came into the room while I was fighting the same people over the same problem that no one could or would solve. After seeing me so upset she said, 'Perhaps it is time for me to take my life now.' I jumped up, kissed her and held her as she cried.

The Hippocratic oath speaks of doing no harm and yet so many individuals who are the cogs in this machine are not required to take any oath whatsoever but they should be, for they are indeed doing grave harm. All of the executives and workers in the insurance and drug companies and in the medical billing offices of doctors and hospitals are somehow excused from the dreadful conduct of the entities they work for, but this is rationalization at its most grotesque. Many of our fellow citizens are like the 'good' Germans now, who follow without thought; the cogs that make the machine work and prosper. They say the predictable things that people engaged in dreadful deeds always say: 'I just work here and I'm following procedures' or 'I have to feed my family' or 'I need to pay my mortgage', as if these needs are any excuse for the brutalization of others.

Sadly, when they or their loved ones cross over to that other bank, as we all will, clarity may finally descend upon them. They will look for kindness and support at their most desperate hour only to find that those around them are the same kinds of people they had once been. It is they who will then be surrounded by the cogs that have taken their places and who will now take everything away. All these workers, our neighbors and friends, are part of the tyranny and in-humanity, for the system itself cannot function without them. We are, in many ways, the disease itself.

Yesterday the hospice nurses were trying to get to Kris, as was the pharmacy, with a delivery of morphine so as to help with her pain. The difficulty was that the nurses and drugs could not reach her until later in the day because of an event here in Monterey and Carmel for the Concours d'Elegance, a fancy auto show of sorts where people with expensive cars smoke cigars, drink, have a grand old time and seemingly accomplish little beyond hedonism. The old trick of mentioning that 'Some proceeds go to charity' is perhaps employed to help assuage any need for self-reflection. It would seem that, in all the carnival planning, the mayor, police chief and city council had made no provisions for a situation like my wife's.

Here in Carmel we all pretend to be what a lot of American towns pretend to be these days: a community. Carmel is not a community. It is an opportunity. The town sells itself cheaply and often, to any salesman trying to sell one thing or another while using the natural beauty of the area as a backdrop, reducing it to a Hollywood set of sorts. As a result, people like my wife simply don't rate any consideration, not even where death is concerned. It does not matter that my wife, an anthropologist, inspired young people in Sierra Leone to become teachers and doctors or that she helped develop and build a well system so children there could have safe drinking water. It does not matter that she is a profoundly modest and kind human being whose friends adore her. Her qualities of humanity and quiet generosity do not matter either. My dear wife had to suffer for the most banal of reasons, because no one, from the police chief to the mayor to the city council and the business people, seemingly gave my wife, or anyone in a similar situation, a passing thought. There was no malice: it is just who they are. And that is dying the American way. It is just who we are.

In a little while I will go back into our small bedroom filled with friends and I will read to Kris, as we have done for each other for over twenty-five years. This morning I was reading to her from Saint-Exupéry's *The Little Prince* when I came to the passage where the fox reveals the secret. It remains a secret only to those with closed hearts who, long ago, forgot that the riches we have always possessed are not the ones we hold in our hands, but are each other.

I think I have come to understand that the quality of a life lived is not determined by the contents of a person's pockets but rather by what is contained in their heart. It is what someone has stood for and how they acted or not upon their humanity that finally informs. The fox is right, for what has always been essential is invisible to the eye and we Americans would do well to remember that.

Kris L. Hardin

1953 ~ 2012

CARMEL.- Kris L. Hardin passed away August 21, 2012 after a courageous five-year battle with brain cancer. During that struggle she displayed grace, kindness and wit to her many friends and family. She never lost her humanity or the love and wonder of life.

Kris was a gifted anthropologist and writer who spent years in Sierra Leone, West Africa, doing fieldwork among the Kono people of Kainkordu. All of that research now resides in the British Library Collection, London. Kris was a talented painter as well who only recently shared with family and friends her many oils and watercolors that were done over nearly a decade.

Kris was born in Fresno, CA on March 7, 1953. Following her undergraduate education, she earned a PhD in anthropology from Indiana University, a Fulbright scholarship and Rockefeller and Smithsonian fellowships.

Over the next 25 years Kris, with her husband, Michael Katakis, collaborated on projects all over the world, producing exhibitions and books derived from her work. Her last book was "Photographs and Words", published by the British Library in 2011. In 1999 Kris was elected "Fellow" of the Royal Geographical Society in London. In 2011 she was presented to Her Majesty, Queen Elizabeth.

Kris was one of those rare and remarkable people blessed with a wide array of talents and with the traits of humility, quiet eloquence and a deep wisdom coupled with a dark, intelligent humor. Her friends were from every walk of life and from around the world. When you were with Kris you simply wanted to just stay.

To the dear friends here, and from around the world who were there when the skies first darkened and then stayed close all through Kris' terrible ordeal, there simply are no words. Finally, to the many health care people, especially Dr. Susan Chang, Dr. Nancy Rubin and Ms. Beverla Miles, who gently cared for Kris and to the selfless and kind Hospice "volunteers" who gave so generously of their time. Thank you all. Your many kindnesses shall not soon be forgotten.

Kris is survived by her mother, Eleanor Hardin of Fresno; her brother, Douglas Hardin, Jr. and her husband, Michael Katakis.

MY TRUE NORTH

Journal entry
29 September 2003
Sounio, Greece

Kris and I have hiked up to the ruins of the Temple of Poseidon and the sea opens up before us. The breathtaking vista makes clear why the temple was built here. If Poseidon, the god of the sea, had lived anywhere he would have lived here. It is magnificent and we are gloriously alone with these ruins created some 440 years before Christ. Kris is sitting on one of the massive overturned columns as she opens her rucksack and pulls out the small watercolor box I bought for her in Paris years before. She is turned sideways and with her large sunbonnet and skirt, in silhouette, she looks like a traveler from another century in one of those old books that you would find in London. From the day I met her, I thought her the most beautiful woman I had ever seen. As a young anthropologist she had just returned from living in West Africa for years. Brains and beauty I had thought at our first meeting when I could not find the words, any words. She was kind as I stumbled. She has always been kind. As I watched her painting, I could not help but think of all of the miles we had traveled together since that first meeting, thousands of miles. I have learned much from her for she is always engaged in the world wanting to understand that which she does not understand. She is my center, my friend and my True North always guiding and welcoming me home.

– M.K.

"Wheresoever she was
there was Eden"

– Mark Twain

Author note: After a brief conversation with someone at Carmel city council, I emailed a copy of this essay and offered them the opportunity to write a rebuttal that would be included verbatim in this volume. No response was ever received.

Jesters do oft prove prophets

Shakespeare, *King Lear*, V, iii

A few days ago I learned of the passing of Gore Vidal. My feelings were first of gratitude and then regret. Gratitude to a man who had unknowingly done me a great service, and regret because my hoped-for visit with him after our exchanges never materialized, due to my responsibilities as caregiver. Time and events conspired against me, and in that instant any possibility of our meeting ended for ever. I shall always regret that.

Years ago, when I was very young and believed that I had already chosen my direction in life, I found myself as a guest on a local television show in Los Angeles. I can still see that sunny afternoon. It was the day that was to confuse and change my life profoundly. At the time I was like many young people, insecure with an air of arrogance, never able to admit that it was merely a mask cloaking my insecurity, even from myself. With that illusion firmly in hand, I was ushered on to a makeshift set that had been constructed outside the station's studio under a stand of trees. I stood behind the cameras, watching the commotion, and then turned to see two men politely discussing the Vietnam War. The men were Gore Vidal and Senator Eugene McCarthy.

As they talked, I was drawn – as a voyeur – into the discussion. I had never heard such conversation. There were words I could not identify and ideas that I struggled to comprehend. The language and pace of the exchange sparkled: it was beautiful. It was as though I was witnessing something from a world far beyond my own. I was.

Senator McCarthy spoke softly and with conviction while Vidal responded with a wit I first mistook for a lack of seriousness. Later, I realized that his was a mordant irony, peppered with facts and knowledge but served in a more palatable and entertaining form. When the talk became more serious and the men began to disagree, the argument remained focused but, oddly, even more convivial and engaging. It was like watching a remarkable dance with music that resonated, so much so that it could change me – and change me it did.

As they continued, I understood for the first time in my short life how much I did not know and how much I wanted to learn. I wanted to recognize those words I had never heard and the ideas I could not understand. I wanted to know more about the people whose names had been woven throughout their conversation, like Socrates and Plato, Hume, Diem and Johnson. I wanted to understand the history of Vietnam, the French and British involvement prior to our own. I wanted to know everything and to dance in conversation as they had done.

The stage director cued me and as I stood waiting I realized, absolutely, that after this brief appearance I would not be going back to the life I had been living just hours before. As you might imagine, I was stunned. How could this be? How could this have happened: my life turned upside down and in less than an hour?

I suppose part of the answer was that I was already in mid-change but had not known what that change would look like or whether I would even recognize the road I must travel when it finally appeared. To be sure, I was hungry for the world in a way I had never been before and sensed there was much to do. I felt that my future was to become uncertain, as futures truly are, while also evolving into some kind of quest, though I did not know for what purpose. It was a pull that suggested something choosing me rather than the other way around and it was terrifying and wonderful at the same time. In hindsight, it felt like what is sometimes referred to as a 'calling'.

It was that afternoon, listening to those two men, that lit the spark that would give my undisciplined mind just a bit more focus. Words and ideas had set fire to my imagination and I have been grateful ever since.

I did not understand then, nor for some time afterwards, that I had been hungry for experiences that would impart to me knowledge, the kind of knowledge that might one day lead to wisdom and restraint. I wanted to understand the world as it was, not just as I wished it to be. After listening to Vidal and McCarthy, I instinctively knew that I could not attempt to make the world or myself better until I saw both as they were. It seems so simple now, but at the time it was a profound awakening for me. What I remember clearly is that, days after the program, I understood that my quest would begin with two things: books and travel. But which books, and travel to where? I decided to begin with the words of Gore Vidal.

There is a quote that Vidal used often, and he used it that day on the set. Quoting Socrates, he said, 'The unexamined life is not worth living.' I began with that challenge and kept it close throughout the following years as if it were a talisman, and so it came to be. Some time later I heard Vidal manipulate the quote to provide a witty but very cutting analysis of present-day America. 'The untelevised life is not worth living,' he said as the people laughed. I found the quote to be very sharp eyed, but in contradiction to his other cheekier dictum, that one should 'never pass up an opportunity to have sex or be on television'. Employing such mordant irony sometimes allowed critics to dismiss him as an entertainer rather than a serious commentator on the American story. That was a mistake.

Vidal possessed a sparkling gift for writing, and for me this is particularly evident in his essays. He had mastered the use of wit and irony, and could always find humour in the most serious of subjects. He was a calculating jester, delivering the worst of medicines wrapped in something that also brought about a smile, at least some of the time. Those who make the error of thinking him a mere provocateur, 'enfant terrible' or witty television personality would do well to read his essays on America: they show a brilliant mind and masterful writer at work. The essays always seemed to me to be written by someone who, despite his masks of wit, occasional cruelty and sometimes outrageous conclusions, also cared deeply for his country. He was both heartbroken and angered by what it had become. If one wants a synthesis of America in the twentieth century, one need only read 'How We Missed the Saturday Dance' to observe a serious intellect in action. Some have written that Vidal was America's Montaigne. I would like to suggest, with apologies to my French friends, that he was better than Montaigne, much better.

Reading Vidal's commentary on September 11, while others at *The New York Times*, *The New Yorker* and other publications were drinking the patriotic Kool-Aid and marching in step with the Bush Administration's fictional narrative, was also to understand something of the man's courage. In his book *Dreaming War*, Gore Vidal wrote:

[The war on terror] ... is an imperial grab for energy resources. ... After 9/11 the country was really shocked and terrified. [Bush] does a little war dance and talks about evil axis and all the countries he's going to go after. And how long it is all going to take, he says with a happy smile, because it means billions and trillions for the Pentagon and for his oil friends. And it means curtailing our liberties, so this is all very thrilling for him. He's right out there reacting, bombing Afghanistan. Well, he might as well have been bombing Denmark. Denmark had nothing to do with 9/11. And neither did Afghanistan, at least the Afghanis didn't.

While I do not always agree with Vidal's opinions or conclusions, I marveled at his courage in saying here what he thought to be true, even at a time when a majority of the country was in opposition to such positions being held, let alone voiced. With the exception of a very few prominent people, like the equally brave Susan Sontag, Vidal was quite fearless and alone in his critical views of the United States and its behavior following the attacks on September 11. Vidal's life seems to have been punctuated with words that were determined to speak truth to power and never more so than after the attacks, a time when many of the American people, hallucinating in their own patriotic delusions, wanted people with questions or opposing views to just shut up and get on the bus. Thankfully, Gore Vidal was never a passive passenger.

What makes Vidal so infuriating to his critics is how often his observations have proved to be correct. What makes him even more infuriating is that, despite being a patrician, it was the wealthy and powerful, the established order, his 'class', as he described them, who were so often his primary targets and the ones he held responsible for what the country had become. He told me as much in our phone conversation.

As my life went on, I was determined that I would attempt to live a life of learning and action and would take Vidal's example and try to be brave with my words. I would travel the world, keep journals, write endless letters and read, read, read. I would ask questions, treat the world with respect and attempt to understand both the good and the bad that I came upon. As much as possible, I did this by abandoning my western perceptions and putting myself in the other guy's shoes. I have done so with varying degrees of success ever since.

The words in the journals mounted and my bags were rarely at rest. I would work late at night in restaurants, washing dishes until I had enough money to leave again. I was learning.

As a result of the person I was becoming, one day, in a crowded university hall, I was able to recognize someone I did not know. I asked a friend if they knew who she was. 'That's Dr. Kris Hardin. She's just returned to the States after years of field work in Africa.' I had met my future wife. She was an anthropologist with the Smithsonian and her work was in Sierra Leone, West Africa. Over the following months we talked of the world and in our conversations, we danced.

In Washington, D.C., during a lull from my clumsy attempts at courting, I decided to go to the Vietnam Veterans Memorial. I was shocked when I found a school friend's name and was deeply shaken by my reaction. My journal entry from that day records my surprise:

At Wall 25, I began to look for Line 91. The black granite reflected my image and I clearly saw my face; then there he was. I stared for a moment, not at his name, but at my reflection. I had changed; my hair had some gray and the lines around my eyes showed experience and wear. I reached out to touch my friend's name and felt my friend was the same, still eighteen. Young people who die are forever frozen in time. Everything around the names will change in time I suppose. The public will come year after year and they will see their reflections in the stone, their graying hair and their bodies aging. They will change and, one day, they will be gone, but all these names will remain as they are, forever. I touched Wayne's name and I began to cry. I cried for a long time and the granite reflected my sadness and release. I was finally able to say good-bye to my friend. I knew he would always be there.

So began a two-and-a-half-year project to photograph and interview people at the Vietnam Veterans Memorial. While working, there was seldom a time that I did not think of something that had been said between those two men long ago. I focused on the legacy of the war, the people left behind, the roads not taken and what it had come to mean years later. I approached the subject with seriousness and resolve but also with a gentle humor, for when talking with surviving family and soldiers I slowly came to understand that all of those wounded souls were in need of something, anything that might, even for a moment, take them away from their attempts to find a peace that would never come.

In the evenings I would go back to Kris and tell her what I had seen and what people had told me. After a year she thought I should approach a publisher. Two years later, my first book was published.

After all this time I am still unable to describe how it felt seeing the first copy. It was as if I had been on the right road, with work, with the woman I loved and with life. I started to think that maybe, just maybe, my work could touch people and perhaps matter in some way. Further books followed, some better than others but all attempting to be something done well and with purpose.

My life of learning progressed: I had been reading carefully, extensively and traveling the world. There was Morocco and West Africa, Cuba, China and Taiwan, the Philippines, Korea, England, France and a journey with my father back to his beginnings on Crete, a place where he had seen such horrible things during World War II and where the secrets were kept. In Spain I spent two days with a man people would describe as a terrorist. He was a member of ETA. I kept an open mind and I learned.

I read Gore Vidal's essays on America and with great sadness I recognized his observations and his conclusions. As ever, his was a sharp eye, a pen that, when angered, gave no quarter and expected none in return. But again and again I detected a melancholy, a wish that things could be different, an unspoken belief that honest, well-thought-out words might inform the country and, with that knowledge, might change its course. Because of that frustrated hopefulness, I have always seen Vidal as a reluctant optimist.

Some years ago I decided to write to Gore Vidal. In that

letter I told him of the program long ago and how it had changed the direction of my life. I told him what I had been reading and where I had traveled and what I thought about a number of things, including the Vietnam War. I wrote about the people I had talked to around the world and the woman I had married. I wrote about how important and helpful his essays had been. I wanted him to know how much I appreciated what he had unknowingly done for me. I wanted to thank him for all of it but words failed to express what I held in my heart. I told him many things, serious and otherwise, personal and general. The letter was long and filled with sentiments, not of idolatry, but of respect, fondness and appreciation.

My wife read the letter, leaning over my shoulder, and said, 'I would so love to receive such a letter. You should send it.' I did not send the letter for another two weeks. I had hoped to find better words, but those words never came. It was time to get on with it.

I knew that Vidal was living in Italy at the time but also had a home in southern California. I contacted an acquaintance in New York who knew Mr. Paul Newman and Ms. Joanne Woodward who, I had been told, were dear friends of Vidal. The acquaintance contacted me and said that they (Newman and Woodward) would either mail the letter directly or hand-deliver it when they visited him soon. I sent a sealed envelope with the letter inside and then made a second letter and sent it to Gore Vidal's attention, Ravello, Italy, along with some of my books.

Some weeks later, while at work, I received a call from my wife saying that a beautiful envelope had arrived.

'It's from Italy,' she said. 'I think it's from Vidal.'

'Open it,' I said, but ever wise, Kris told me that she wanted me to see the letter as she saw it now.

'Forgive me, dear, but I want the pleasure of seeing you open it. I want to watch the expression on your face.'

That evening I sat at the kitchen table staring at the little envelope. It was beautiful thin paper, pale blue in color, and the Italian stamp spoke of a life far away. My name appeared to have been written by an older, unsteady hand. I lingered as I moved my fingers across the stamp. Kris passed me the letter opener.

The letter itself was written on paper even thinner than the envelope and was both delicate and strong. This was a letter writer's paper.

'Go on, read it,' Kris pressed.

His words were direct and kind, funny and intelligent. Mr. Vidal thanked me for my letter. He told me that what I had done thus far was something to be proud of and then suggested, because of some of the conclusions I had reached, that I could now use the four greatest words in the English language: 'I told you so.'

He went on to say that I had followed, to a wide degree, one of my ancestor's dictums that 'The unexamined life is not worth living.' There was Socrates again. The letter was handwritten and welcoming and he was very kind. I put it down and looked up to see Kris smiling.

'What a lovely letter. I love you and I'm so very proud of you.' Kris was always like that.

Life went on, with more writing and travel, and I took to writing more letters and getting lovely paper to write them on. Maybe being a better letter writer would make me a better writer, I thought.

A few years later a friend told me that Vidal had left Italy and was living in California. He suggested that I call him. He told me that Vidal preferred people to fax him with their number. He would then choose whether or not to respond. And so I sent a fax, one sunny California afternoon, and after about twenty minutes the phone rang. I immediately recognized the voice on the line.

Our conversation began as if it were a continuation of some past discussion. We spoke of the recent election of George W. Bush. 'Oh, Katakis, the greatest criminal class in US history has just ascended the White House.' We debated that a bit and then moved on to John F. Kennedy's assassination, which I had studied in detail. We talked about Tennessee Williams, Hiroshima and then Vietnam. He seemed delighted when we discussed literature and I told him how much I thought of Italo Calvino's work.

We talked on and in a moment I realized that our conversation sparkled and, even though he led, we were dancing. Our conversation seemed effortless and the words used I now understood and the ideas discussed were my ideas as well, for I had learned a few steps of my own. Back and forth we went, ending with the mutual hope that some time soon I would travel down to his home in Hollywood. It was not to be. We never spoke again, but the dance lingered. It lingers still.

His was a voice that amused, informed, infuriated, scolded, reminded and asked repeatedly for people to remain conscious and to think for themselves. That was Gore Vidal's dance and for a few moments, on a single day, he let me join in and it was wonderful. So, *merci, adieu* and thanks for the dance, Mr. Vidal.

Man is the Reasoning Animal. Such is the
claim. I think it is open to dispute ...
Man is the Religious Animal. He is the only
Religious Animal. He is the only animal that
has the True Religion – several of them.

Mark Twain, 'The Lowest Animal' (1897)

In 1999 the anthropologist Kris L. Hardin wrote, 'Increasingly
in the United States a large percentage of the American people
are adopting an attitude that says, I shall see it when I believe
it. This is not only tragic, it is dangerous.'

At first glance this statement seems merely a clever play on
words but upon reflection it becomes apparent that Dr.
Hardin was concerned as to how a society should proceed and
evolve when an increasing percentage of the population dis-
regards facts and evidence that do not coincide with their
beliefs and superstitions. This is dangerous indeed, for a society can absorb a small percentage of such ignorance, but
cannot endure if a majority of people hold to such views.

The question becomes self-evident. How do we communicate

with each other if facts and evidence are no longer a serious part of the discourse, and are replaced instead with uninformed opinions which are used not to convince but, rather, to trick and coerce? In such an environment how does one reach an informed position or build consensus or even know which questions to ask?

We have seen and heard of such things throughout history. Institutional ignorance once demanded that Galileo recant that which he had discovered to be true. However, despite Galileo's enforced retraction and the Inquisition's banning of his writings, the fact still remained that the earth revolved around the sun and not the other way around. This is the fundamental problem with 'extreme' believers throughout human history. They are almost always obstructive in the evolution of thought and when proven wrong they become more self-righteous, demanding ever more obedience, not for the sake of knowledge but for their own power.

America in 2012 is awash in extreme beliefs and believers. There are some who believe that vitamins can cure everything and those who believe that Evolution is a lie. Some believe, without a doubt, and in spite of evidence to the contrary, that Fox News is really news, or that global warming is a hoax. We see people who steer their lives based on the belief that the world will end on a specific day and others who believe that Newt Gingrich has something to teach us about morality. There are those who believe that no matter how ill someone becomes they should just wait, pray and God will cure. Wouldn't it be nice to think so? I wish them luck. Some believers think that President Obama is not an American, while others think Donald Trump matters. Many still believe that Saddam Hussein was involved in the attacks of September 11 or that the United States went to Iraq to 'free' the Iraqi people.

And then there are the varied 'devout' among us who are not content with their faith alone, but also feel compelled to inform others of 'God's Truth' as they see it, in order to save the rest of us. We have Scientologists who believe in L. Ron Hubbard (enough said) and Mormons who believe in some very curious things that may, at first, seem humorous, until of course one of them is running for the presidency of the United States. The trouble we have in America is not intolerance but the tolerance of the intolerant and intolerable by the enlightened.

We have so many believers now that it is hard to get away from them. They have injected themselves into business and public policy. They attempt to take books deemed inappropriate from library shelves and then try to place creationist doctrine (Intelligent Design) in the classroom to give a 'balanced' counterpoint to Evolution, never accepting that one is predicated on evidence while the other is simply belief sold as truth. And then there are the pharmacists and doctors who believe that they can deny a woman certain drugs or treatment because of their own beliefs. For those kinds of persons I wish a number of things. Luck isn't one of them.

The believers come to your home uninvited so as to convince you of their faith (or product) and to remind you, with a touch of fire and brimstone, that even though there are many beliefs, theirs alone is the 'true path'. All extreme believers possess this irony, whether they realize it or not.

Even though some religious doctrine instructs that we should not judge lest we be judged, the extreme American believers are rabid judges who are judging others all of the time. Even worse, many are selective moralists of the type that argue for the rights of a fetus on the one hand and for capital punishment on the other. This is the kind of moral jujitsu that is practiced not by critical thinkers, but by zealots.

You can always tell an American extremist for they all use the word 'but' in their initially rational discussions, which go something like this:

'Did you hear about Dr. so-and-so, who was shot in the back of his head in his church yesterday?' (This happened by the way.)

'Yes, I did, and it's horrible. I feel badly for his family.'

'Oh yes, it's a terrible thing and just think of his poor children and wife, it's just terrible,' (get ready now) 'but you know he was an abortion doctor. He was in a dangerous job. He was involved in the killing of a lot of children.' (Yes, someone did say this to me.)

'What he was doing was legal and they were not children according to the law and you aren't justifying murder, are you?'

'Oh no, I would never condone murder, but' (yes, again) 'I'm just saying.'

It seems that the believing extremists in America and elsewhere have similar doctrines that demand the relinquishing of moderation and reason. What all of the extremist Christians, Jews, Muslims and others have in common is their fear and hatred of reason itself. They have, whether they know it or not, adopted a portion of Martin Luther's 'Sermon on the Gospel of Saint John' where that old extremist himself preached, 'Whoever wants to be a Christian must be intent on silencing the voice of reason.'

And here we arrive at the crux of some kinds of power. It is hard to hold power when people think for themselves and engage in that sin of sins, questioning. And yet, it is odd to think that the great god in the sky would give to human beings the ability to reason but condemn them when they choose to employ it. It's confusing, isn't it? But then it would seem that only the 'enlightened' are confused by such contradictions and hypocrisy. Extreme believers are never confused and that's what makes them so dangerous to a civilized or developing society.

In America these believers are increasingly involved in politics, overtly and covertly altering public policy, imposing their beliefs in a way that affects people's lives, for the 'true' American believers, like their brethren elsewhere, want you to believe as well, with the proviso that what you believe is what they believe.

The believers I speak of gut a society from within and always follow a tried and tested pattern. To get more attention and to solidify loyalty, there must be enemies of their faith and of the state, who they can point to and blame for the perceived societal ills of the moment. It's the Jews one century and homosexuals the next, or immigrants, or people who do not look the same or talk or pray the same. Society becomes fractionalized to the point that the people eventually look upon each other with suspicion and fear or as mere commodities to be exploited. It is fatiguing, I know, but there is a cure. It is doubt.

There are the searchers among us, the enlightened, and they are from every walk of life. They question their beliefs and retain an open mind. Their morality is predicated not by a list of institutional rules followed without question, but upon a sense of social justice, knowledge and inquiry. These questioners take seriously the Socratic dictum that 'The unexamined life is not worth living' or the aphorism 'Know thyself'. They realize, profoundly so, that to possess doubt is to be open to the world and to have blind faith is, well, to be blind.

The enlightened are attempting to find grace, not in the hereafter, but in the here and now, in the lives and struggles of the people in this life, and from that knowledge they hone their beliefs with an informed perception of the world as it is while also working for a better world that might be. They epitomize Gandhi's suggestion to 'Be the change you wish to see in the world'.

These enlightened searchers come from every background and philosophy. They are the best of us. They are priests and nuns, Atheists and Muslims, Buddhists, Jews and Hindus. They are shopkeepers and presidents, street sweepers and bakers and maybe even the old woman you passed on the street today.

They are large in numbers and comprise the most inclusive of fraternities. The price of admission is a modicum of doubt and a mind poised to change based upon the evidence. To do otherwise is to submit to the tragic self-limitation that George Orwell alluded to in *1984* when he wrote, 'Orthodoxy is not thinking, not needing to think. Orthodoxy is unconsciousness.'

This is a remarkable world in spite of the difficulties we all face and the United States can be a remarkable country, but not by power and belief alone. To embrace doubt is to be freed from suffocating ideologies that promote fear and do little more than hold back people's potential and, dare I say, joy.

I prefer to be conscious, to question and to be with people who think, search and discover. All these things are important, but really it is also so much more fun to let go of the arrogant view that we know all, and thus knowing all, need not go further. For me, I wish to see what is around the next corner. I love surprises.

That's what careless words do. They make people love you a little less.

Arundhati Roy, *The God of Small Things* (1997)

In one of his films, the great American philosopher Clint Eastwood plays a character who suggests that a man should know his limitations. It is unfortunate then that Mr. Eastwood did not heed his character's advice before addressing the Republican convention in Tampa, Florida.

The day after his speech I went for my early-morning walk along the ocean in Carmel, California. As I stared at Point Lobos in the distance, a woman I did not know, and had not seen approach, struck up a conversation by rather giddily asking if I had 'watched' Eastwood's speech.

'Did you see Clint's speech last night?'

'Yes, I did.'

'Wasn't it great? What did you think?'

'Well, if Mr. Eastwood ever feared that he would be seen as

a gracious, kind and thoughtful man, he need not fear that any longer.'

'Are you criticizing Clint Eastwood? You can't do that.'

'I beg your pardon?'

'You can't criticize him. He's done a lot for the community.'

I found this statement rather odd because the woman did not seem as if she was from the area. Her accent suggested the Midwest.

'What has he done for the "community"?'

'Lots of stuff.'

'Well, I can see how Jesus Christ got started, but I have never been a good apostle for anyone. I'm curious, madam, if you were given the opportunity to speak to three or four hundred million people, would you not fret and reflect about what you might say? Would you not want to appeal to people's better angels or speak to Americans seriously, perhaps suggesting we should work together in spite of our differences for the benefit of the most vulnerable of our citizens? Would you not talk about how such a pursuit was not only possible, but noble and kind and simply the right thing to do?

'Instead, Mr. Eastwood chose to joke about things being shoved up people's rectums while in the Republican hall the good "family value" Christians cheered him on, children in hand. No, I did not like his speech, for it showed what I believe is the worst of us and further demonstrated that we are not in this together.'

Since Eastwood's performance and that early-morning exchange I have been haunted by the idea of opportunities not merely missed, but thrown away. Opportunities to speak to each other on a higher and more thought-provoking level; opportunities to be more kind and generous for the sake of those virtues alone; opportunities to look deeper into ourselves and to question our own motives and desires.

Eastwood's vulgar joking appeared to be more about his ego than anything else, and there was a carelessness in his words that seemed a metaphor for the country itself; but then I realized it was no mere metaphor, but an attitude increasingly enveloping the land and the people, an attitude borne of indifference and an absence of critical thinking. This kind of carelessness seems to be surrounding us these days and, as the Republican convention recently demonstrated, is being applauded as well.

Since that night I have thought about what I would have said if someone had given me the extraordinary opportunity to address millions of people. I would have been terrified, of course — not for myself but for my words. I would have wanted them to mean something, to express how much I cared, not just for America and Americans but for the world and its people and how we are all connected on this planet. I would have reminded the people and myself that our lives are short and that, to do good, they must involve the virtues of kindness, generosity and empathy.

Perhaps I would have referred to Thomas Paine and said that the world was my country and that my religion was to do good, or I would have tried to convince people on all sides of the political and cultural spectrum that in spite of all of our differences, perhaps we could agree that poverty is a scourge, or that corporations, while being allowed to do business, should not be allowed a larger voice than that of a single citizen or be able to corrupt the basic foundations of our government. I would have asked if we could agree that while business and jobs are important, they alone do not define us and I would have tried to find a way to ask the believers among us to consider employing a bit more doubt and humility in their sometimes rather unyielding beliefs. I would have pleaded that we not destroy people's lives simply because they have had the misfortune of becoming ill. I would have suggested that if we could agree in principle about these things then surely, as a good and decent people, we could find a way to make those same things a reality for the benefit of all Americans, as has been done at other times in our past.

I would have fretted and worried over my words because I would have wanted them to convey my respect for my fellow citizens and to express my sense of responsibility to the rest of the world.

One day, as I rushed across the parking lot toward the local hospital's entrance, I saw a familiar face approaching. It was Clint Eastwood. I had heard some days before that his mother was very ill and possibly close to death. As he came closer, I could see that he was sad.

Our eyes met and I said, 'Hello. I hope things are okay.'

He said hello, smiled a sad smile and nodded.

As I entered the hospital, I gave a last passing thought to Mr. Eastwood, not because he was a celebrity but because he was a fellow human being who seemed terribly worried about someone he loved and heartbroken at the thought of losing them. I wished him well.

Over a year later it was I who was rushing to the hospital, terrified that I might lose someone that I dearly loved. As my wife and I went through those first terrible months, I thought back to that chance meeting in the hospital parking lot the year before and wondered if people like Mr. Eastwood ever thought about people like my wife and me, about what we have gone through and how afraid we Americans are at being taken advantage of or harmed in our darkest hour by entities that see numbers, not people, and who control more and more of our lives. I wondered if he ever wished people like us well.

I had assumed the answer was yes but sadly, after listening to Mr. Eastwood's careless words, delivered to many in the hall who represented the very business entities that have caused so much harm, it felt to me as though he never gave people like my wife a second's thought.

If true, how sad, all those opportunities and kindnesses thrown away. In spite of his careless words I still wish Mr. Eastwood well, partly because to do otherwise would be to lose a bit of my own humanity.

5 REMAINING SEATED

> I wish they would just take me as I am.
>
> Vincent van Gogh, in a letter to
> his brother Theo van Gogh

The Smithsonian letter

16 December 2010

Dr. G. Wayne Clough
Secretary of the Smithsonian
Smithsonian Institution
P.O. Box 37012
MRC 016
Washington D.C. 20013-7012

Dear Dr. Clough,

I have thought long and hard before writing this letter but there are times when the hypocrisy rises to just below one's chin, then one either does something about it or drowns in it. I have chosen not to drown.

Sadly, I must tell you now why I am making a formal request that my photographic portrait of Maya Lin, that was acquired by the National Portrait Gallery for its collection some years ago, be returned to me immediately for I can no longer have my work in an institution such as yours.

Over the last week I have watched and listened with great interest and an open mind, to the varying opinions regarding the removal of Mr. Wojnarowicz's video installation titled *Fire in My Belly* that was part of the National Portrait Gallery's Hide/Seek exhibition over the last six weeks.

I had hoped in the ensuing days that a satisfying editorial rationale would be put forward explaining why the piece suddenly did not fit into the exhibition it had been part of since the exhibition's inception, or for that matter, any compelling artistic argument as to why the art in question was now unsuitable for the show.

No such reasons were given but what has become disturbingly clear is that the National Portrait Gallery has removed the 'questionable' art, from an ongoing exhibition, not because of the work's merit or lack thereof, or for that matter large scale protests (which would be no justification for removal) but because some small-minded bigots and solipsistic careerists expressed offense at something in the exhibition.

The charges of religion being insulted or his vilifying of Jews and homosexuals seem to always be Mr. Donohue's modus operandi in getting attention. Is it this man that you were so afraid of, so much so, that you took down an installation of a work in an exhibition at the National Portrait Gallery?

Sir, you have made a horrific decision and betrayed a trust that was not yours to give away. It was your job to stand up against the bullies and book burners and those who would decide what we see and read and say. It was your job to stand firm.

As a very frightened little boy I remember being taken to a Chicago Library. The kindly librarian saw that I was very scared and no doubt my father had informed her that back in our small apartment my mother was dying. The librarian walked around her large desk and put her arm around my shoulder and then walked me through the towering shelves of books and then she said:

Every word in all of these books is a thread that will weave a magic carpet that will take you everywhere and after you have traveled through these pages you will find that there are more kind and open hearts than there are monsters and knowing that will make you less afraid.

Over the next few years my father and the librarian directed me to the world. There was *Kim*, and Mark Twain, who described racism so well that I began to understand the cruelty that I was seeing in the streets of Chicago in regard to the treatment of black people. I read the *Arabian Nights* and later *Mein Kampf,* which made me want to know more about WWII and how a nation could follow such a monster.

The librarian and my father were not protecting me from the world but rather introducing it to me with balance and context and knowledge. What they did was to show me the whole of the world and of human conduct and that just led to more questions and reading and then understanding.

I never knew if the librarian was right or left, gay or straight, religious or not. What I do know however is that she took the trust that had been placed in her hands seriously but, at her core I now believe what she cherished above all things were the rights of expression. To read and write and think and speak what one wished even if those words or ideas offended others. She realized then, as I do now, that the hope for us all resided on those shelves and in those volumes and she guarded them for the majority of her life I suspect.

I am so sorry that you felt that you could not rise to the level of that small, magnificent neighborhood librarian and I really don't care what claims of political pressures were placed upon you or the threats which, I'm sure, were made regarding funding by the little elected cultural blackmailers. You should have called the little bullies' bluff, for the bully is never satiated when one capitulates, only emboldened.

I am sorry that I have had to write this letter and

regret its tone, but sir, you have done something horrific,
something that has been the currency of despots in other
societies. You have taken away someone's voice. And
when the time came for you to stand and say no to the
blackmailers and zealots you remained seated and for
this reason I cannot have my work in the possession of
your institution.

Regretfully,
Michael Katakis

After receiving the above letter, the National Portrait Gallery
refused to reinstate Mr. Wojnarowicz's work to the exhibition
or return my portrait of Maya Lin. The portrait remains in the
institution's collection. I have cut all ties with the NPG.

OTHER VOICES

(in discussion with Michael Katakis)

AM It's bigger, that's for sure, but not necessarily better. You're great but I wonder how you get in such debt, though, and it's hard for me to know what your priorities are. I meet a lot of Americans in my work and they are wealthy and seem educated but they don't seem to know anything about the world, anything outside of America. Believe me, most don't even know their own [phone] country code. They're very nice but they don't seem to know the world.

MK Of all the cultures that you work with and all of the people from different parts of the world that you come in contact with, which among them, in regard to nationality, seem to be most uninformed about the world?

AM Americans.

AM, concierge (male, Australian, 33)
Australia

[In America] All things are possible.

> Alizé Le Maoult, film-maker (female, French, age unknown)
> Paris, France

MK You have told me that you are in America illegally and that you have come for opportunity, for work, but please tell me, if you are cheated or taken advantage of, what do you do? If you are abused at work or elsewhere, where do you go?

AL I go nowhere.

> AL, farmworker (female, Mexican, 33)
> Salinas, California

You guys are very positive thinkers.

> LD, waitress (female, British, 21)
> Paris

The United States is a beautiful country where everything is possible and where even rascals can be turned into heroes.

> ED, teacher, translator and fortune-teller (female, French, 32)
> Paris, France

You [the United States] are like children, man. Teenagers that have angered the 'grandfather' [the Middle East], that's who you are, and now there is a price to pay. Charity, brother, you must practice true charity and love.

> S, taxi driver (male, Lebanese, approx. 59)
> Sydney, Australia

America is superficial, pretentious, insincere. Good for the rich or if you know someone; if not, then not so good.

Adriana S, 'wannabe student without friends' (female, Italian-born Australian, 20)
Melbourne, Australia

(Despite the description that she gave of herself, I found Adriana a very charming and intelligent young woman with a dark sense of humor that suggested a street-smart sophistication.)

You have to change the system and get the world's sympathy back. America today is wrong politics. You must change. If America gets better the world gets better, maybe.

Franco C, restaurant owner (male, Italian, 61)
Melbourne, Australia

I would say that the Americans I met face to face were salt of the earth but very much black and white as regards political ideas, especially about the rest of the world. Perhaps their understanding of democracy wouldn't fit the ideal of other western countries – but then no one is perfect.

PM, priest, Holy Ghost missionary (male, Irish, 78)
Woorabinda, Queensland

In my opinion the downfall taking place in the US which is reconcilable is that we have lost our ability to think critically.

WJMC, entrepreneur (male, American, 23)
Paris, France

6 BRINGING BACK THE DRAFT: A MORAL IMPERATIVE

> Mr. Brady has done something to bring home
> to us the terrible reality and earnestness of
> war. If he has not brought bodies and laid
> them in our dooryards and along the streets,
> he has done something very like it.
>
> *The New York Times*, October 20, 1862
> Reporting on Matthew Brady's New York
> exhibit concerning the Civil War dead,
> one month after the Battle of Antietam

If war, any war, is essential to a nation's survival then we cannot turn away. We must look it in the eye and see exactly what we are paying for and what the price will be. Furthermore, it would seem that every citizen's life should be engaged and disrupted by something so grave that it requires we send our sons and daughters to die and to kill other people's children.

To be sure there have been times in our history when such a shared sacrifice was justified in places far away, for monsters do exist. But sometimes the monsters to be fought are in fact sitting right beside us, and it is important to know them when they appear, even when they are ourselves.

I am here to declare myself an advocate and volunteer for a draft that demands participation by people seventy-five years of age and younger. In good conscience how could it be otherwise, when such a serious endeavor is being considered? You in the wheelchair, you're coming, too, and the blind man over there. Yep, here, let me help you on the bus, for even though you are blind, you have a voice that might comfort frightened boys and girls who are being asked to grow up too quickly.

I am aware that not everyone will actually be able to engage in combat, but they can push a broom or serve food to weary troops and in so doing could make us what Americans today seem desperate to avoid being: in it together. We would feel together, share the pain together and we would die and sacrifice our children together. No escape hatch for the rich or the politician's child. Oh, you're at university? Tough, you're coming as well. Because we've been told this mission is that important, so you will be part of it and if necessary you will die for it too.

The other reason that I strongly advocate for this draconian, yet morally correct draft is that it could be one of the most effective tools against careless and quick war, the likes of which we have seen much of over the last decade, and before. It may also serve to inoculate citizens against arbitrary actions and empty speeches that too often have excited us into war. The possibility of such a quick conflict becomes more problematic when you, who are about to cheer it on, come to the realization that it will be your own ass, or that of a loved one, on the line. Disability and death have a way of focusing the mind – much like a diagnosis of cancer. One moment your life is your own and the next your destiny is not what you had always imagined it to be.

Just as Mr. Brady used his photographs of the Civil War dead to force people to see the true face of war, the draft I propose would hollow out the speeches from the 'dogs of war' and make war itself much harder to sell. Because it should be hard to sell. Very hard. If we must engage in an 'essential' and 'grave' cause – one so important that we must kill and die for it – then all our lives should be suspended and collectively engaged in service to it.

And that is where we find ourselves today: in a so-called war that has gone on longer than World War I and II combined, and in which less than 1 per cent of the American population serves. As of this writing, years after we were told how important the cause and how short and inexpensive the war would be, Americans are still killing and being killed on behalf of a nation which has, some time ago, moved on. To walk the streets of America and to watch the television or listen to the radio, you would not know that a war for our 'very existence' is raging in the Middle East, in a place that many Americans cannot identify on a map. All this killing and dying for such a serious and noble cause goes on while Republican politicians try, over and over again, to get ever more tax breaks for the rich among us. This is rather odd coming from the party of God, country and patriotism. Shared sacrifice indeed.

These days the only way we can tell that a war is going on at all is by the occasional photograph or quick television bite of another flag-draped coffin arriving from a faraway place back to families in little American towns that most Americans cannot find on a map. I wonder, how do you tell someone that their loved one died for nothing and for a country and people that has given them nothing in return, not even sincerity, when they parrot the oft-repeated mantra: 'I'm so sorry for your loss. Your child was a hero and we so appreciate their service and are thankful for it.'

This insincere mantra is of course utter bullshit. To die for a cause that begins with a lie does not make one a hero as much as a victim. The reality is that 'our' sons and daughters, not to mention the sons and daughters of others, are commodities who are used up and damaged or killed. Harsh, I know, but it is time for Americans to look at ourselves without our convenient rose-colored glasses and speeches comprised of false words meant to rationalize, deceive and coerce. Instead we should be saying, 'I am so sorry and ashamed that your family has been put through this and that I have been indifferent and remained silent for so long.'

This is what we have done and this is what we are doing still. How do I know this? I know this because the flag-draped coffins still arrive in small American towns with names I've never heard of and I still don't know what they are dying for.

I know that Americans do not care because the streets of

America are silent and empty of protest. Where are the massive crowds with anger that cannot be quelled or the endless conversations about the war in cafés with talk of what should be done or how we, the people, can help?

I travel all the time and I listen to conversations in parks and bars and offices and I walk down hundreds of American streets. That is how I know we don't think of this and that is how I know we don't care.

To feel bad about something is to have done nothing at all. In our self-righteousness we Americans have actually come to believe that by merely feeling bad about something, we have then done our part. My friends on the left and in the Democratic Party are overwhelmingly subject to this particular malady.

There are times when you gather together and sing 'Kumbaya' and others when you march in the streets and demand that which must be done or halted. We are not doing that because we are not in this together and nothing short of the 'draft' will change that, because we do not care for one another enough for it to be otherwise. We must have a new motivation, something that Americans understand. Self-interest.

The people who die in service of this country now do so without the respect, love and consideration that should have been afforded to them in the first place. They are used carelessly from the beginning and they die for a lie and it is so heartbreaking to say this, but it is true and it continues to be. People instinctively know this.

Since the introduction of an all-volunteer military, I have seen one of the darkest and uglier parts of the American character rise and show itself. It is the face of indifference: cruelty, selfishness and carelessness all wrapped together in a shallow and insincere patriotism that demands pretty, insincere words rather than sacrifice. I have come to despise it, for those pretty words meant to assuage one's guilt or unease are now dripping with blood.

The way we treat and look at this army goes to the heart of our hypocrisy and makes a mockery of our lofty pronouncements concerning justice, fairness and gratitude and it is one of our greatest shames. Quite simply we have lied to ourselves and to them and to each other over and over again, for over a decade now, and we continue to do so as the body counts rise and families, ours and others, suffer. Is it not yet enough?

America is divided on almost every front imaginable. The young don't see why they should have to contribute to Social Security to help older citizens and those senior citizens don't understand why young people complain about the cost of health insurance. The middle classes see people who aren't doing as well as themselves as deficient in some way, while the poor see those above them as exploiters. You see politicians fighting for the rich while a war devastates the economy – not to mention the soul – of the nation, and from the beginning of the war, tax breaks for the wealthy have steadily contributed to the erosion of the essential workings of what remains of this plutocracy disguised as a representative republic. We have betrayed so much.

We are, as if a thousand shards of glass, not binding each other's wounds but in fact the cause of them, with our unkind judgments, indifference and grotesque belief that business, above all things, must be allowed free license to do what it likes, even in the case of war and death, so as to provide 'jobs' which has become the primary buzzword in the 'big con'. The loss of our humanity is speedy and apparent to anyone who listens and observes. It is in the way we eat and the way we speak and in the way we change words so as to rationalize away something that is truly horrible. Torture becomes 'Enhanced Interrogation' while the murder of innocent civilians evolves into 'Collateral Damage'.

I have often wondered how we Americans would have felt if, after the attacks in New York, with all their accompanying death and misery, Bin Laden had contacted the world media. I have imagined him trying to explain that the real target had been the White House and Congress and the Pentagon but, through a series of mistakes, New York had been hit. How would we have reacted if the madman had gone on to apologize for the mistake, to say how regrettable it was, but also to say how much he hoped that the American people would understand that these things happen in war and sometimes innocent people die as 'Collateral Damage'. What would we Americans think after that odd, unapologetic apology, especially if Bin Laden, after his mea culpa, had offered $1500 to each family of those who had perished.

I think we, and the world, know how Americans would have taken it and how much murder would have been in our hearts and it would be understandable; but, as Americans, we seem only to understand that reaction for ourselves, for when 'we' kill other people's innocent families we relegate their loved ones' fate to a mere mistake of conflict followed by monetary compensation which reduces their loved one's memory to that of a cash transaction. And then, after playing the good guys, we seem confused when those people are not grateful for such gestures or for the kind words expressed which they know to be insincere.

I wonder, when did we forget the simple, elegant 'Golden Rule'? Treat others as you would wish to be treated. We can't remember or feel that because we are losing our humanity, even when it comes to the treatment of our own people, which is why, finally, we will not win whatever we think we are supposed to win.

Oh, it's for our security you say, for the protection of the American people and our way of life. I've been hearing that for years and I know, as do most Americans, it is not true. If the mission really were about the safety of the American people, of our way of life, then should we not also be at war with the internal enemies who are killing tens of thousands of Americans every year and ruining the lives of thousands, if not millions, of others?

The soft terrorists in suits and ties in tall buildings who press the computer keys that deny someone's health insurance claim in order to maximize profit – are they not the enemy and a threat to the American people's safety and well-being? The brokerage firms and banks that have consumed billions of dollars, leaving retirees with nothing, while those who stole, legally and otherwise, remain untouched and in full possession of the riches they stole from a million broken dreams – are they not enemies of the people's way of life?

Do we not see such people and institutions as enemies because many of us profit from those very institutions and individuals? If so, what can we say to ourselves then? What can we say to our children and how can we live lives of such base behavior cloaked within elevated words that assist in our denial, and for how long? When does the weight of hypocrisy become too much to bear? I don't know.

The man at the factory making the munitions for the war that is a lie collects his check and goes home to his family and justifies his actions by saying, 'I have to put food on the table for my wife and children.' The investor who invests in the companies of war justifies his great profits from death by telling himself either that he is a patriot doing his part or that, after making a great deal of money from such investments, he can then take a 'portion' of that money and put it towards good works.

Since the war began I cannot remember how many times I have heard, from my conservative friends in particular, the comment, 'Well, those people knew what they were signing up for. It's their job after all.' This response comes after I have expressed how terrible and unjust I find the multiple and repeated deployments and the length of the war itself. One man actually told me that war was good business and then told me about his investments. What are we to do with such indifference from so many quarters, both liberal and conservative? Again, I don't know.

'Those people' the man referred to are us, but so is the child who lives anywhere in the world. Everyone is ours and we are everyone's. We must reclaim a higher ground of morality and charity in our minds and hearts first. It begins with what and how we think. Without that, I simply do not know what winning means.

When I am in the United States, I live in an area populated by a military facility and I have come to know a number of fine and lovely military people and their families. They are a tribe of sorts, watching out for each other in a way we do not watch out for them. Most I have met are intelligent and dedicated young people who are trying to raise families and live a life of purpose and I have found them to be polite, serious and funny, with some being the best of us.

When I have asked some of these bright young military people who General Smedley Butler was, I am usually greeted with a blank expression. At the last count only one person seemed to have a passing recognition of the name and I have found that odd seeing that General Butler, a marine general, was one of the most decorated soldiers in US history with two Congressional Medals of Honor. But then again, it is not so odd, for the General broke the military code of omertà by writing a book and telling the truth.

In General Butler's *War is a Racket*, published in 1935, it is clear that he has had enough of the business of war. He refers to himself as having been 'a high class muscle man for Big

Business, for Wall Street and the bankers. In short, I was a racketeer ... for capitalism.' He writes about those who profited from the first world war and describes the system of procurement and how some of his fellow Americans engaged, not on the battlefield, but in back rooms for ever larger government contracts that would have them produce many times more material than was needed, thus elevating profits to levels previously unimaginable. The General was sick of it all, I suppose, and the weight of the hypocrisy finally had his walls fall down.

General Butler is not known because he has been written out of the American narrative. Like Mr. Brady, Butler told the other story of war, the one that is non-fiction, and in so doing he became something inconvenient and worse to those in the back rooms of every generation making their not so little, unseemly deals. What is so striking about the General's book is how current it reads. It is almost a letter from the past informing us about our present and future, and it is profoundly disturbing to see how successful 'the lie' has been and for how long. Is it not yet enough?

I simply do not know what to do for I feel bad, very bad, about the young people returning in flag-draped coffins and for the others who are broken and will never be the same and I know feeling badly does nothing and means nothing. I think I shall never be able to look these young people in the eye, for I too am part of the betrayal, one of the cogs in the machine that pays the taxes that are then used to purchase the weapons for the next essential and grave cause.

However, I have come to understand that what is truly essential to the well-being of this nation and the security of its people is to put an end to our self-delusions. The only way I can see to elicit such a change is to initiate a draft that all people will have to reflect upon when that letter arrives at their door, ordering them to report to the new life which is no longer their own. Maybe, just maybe, then, together we shall stand and in one voice say, 'Yes, that is enough.'

7 CHRISTOPHER HITCHENS AND THE HEROES THAT NEVER WERE

> I am not always good and noble. I am the
> hero of this story, but I have my off moments.
>
> P.G. Wodehouse, *Love Among the Chickens* (1906)

Journal entry

3 November, 2010
University of California Medical Center
San Francisco, California

I'm in room 805 where Kris is resting after undergoing her third brain operation in eight months for what started out as a brain tumor.

Over the last few days I have been reading Christopher Hitchens' memoir, *Hitch 22*, which is moving, substantive and, as always with Hitchens, well written.

As I watch my wife sleeping, I am well aware that Hitchens, too, is struggling for his life and it makes me sad for I like the man's spirit and intelligence as he stands up for those who get pushed around. It is not all roses however, for even though I have learned much from this intelligent man, I also have a serious quarrel with his conduct leading up to the Iraq war and afterwards.

This self-described Marxist poses in one photograph in the book holding a gun with 'Saddam's enemies' in Kurdistan and in another with the likes of Paul Wolfowitz in Iraq. I find it disturbing that this man of sizable talents used his intellect and powerful words to enable a lie. After reading his memoir, I can see how it happened but still cannot find a satisfying rationale or excuse for such decisions.

At one time I thought Hitchens just a 'celebrity adventurer' or a solipsistic opportunist but he is much deeper, more moral and brave than that. His heroes, if I can call them that, are also mine: Orwell, Sassoon and Owen among others and, based on what he has written, men from England like his father, who fought in WWII with stoicism and humility only to be betrayed by his country when he was no longer of any use. Being an American I am well acquainted with betrayal and understand completely what he is referring to. I have come to believe that his morality is based upon a certain time that is perceived by him as a moral time, or more accurately, a time of actionable morality (really the only kind).

I have always despised and share Hitchens' great aversion to the bully. Unfortunately, I also share what I perceive as his romantic bent toward the adventurer type, the type that wishes to fight in noble battles and die for a just cause. He has said as much in a recent interview on National Public Radio. It is because of those very views and traits that I believe he was pulled into the 'great con' that so many of our shared heroes warned us about. And this is what is so odd. Hitchens writes so movingly about his father being betrayed by a new British government but also by a new ethic, or lack of one, where more and more of England was being privatized and the hills and countryside were being cut up for those contemptuous people who 'made' money rather than 'earned' it. In other words he and his father were watching not merely the breaking up of their country but the destruction of an ethic that had sustained the country through its most difficult days. Why he did not see that the Bush people and others, like the private war contractors who fucked and killed and made bushels of money, were the very same kinds of people, only more rapacious, who had betrayed his father years before, I do not know. What will always remain a mystery to me is how such a brilliant individual could not see how the bully was being replaced by the bullies. Of course, the most unthinkable but highly plausible possibility is that Hitchens did know and took it upon himself to choose what he thought was a lesser of two evils. If so, I wonder what he thought when the atrocities and torture at the hands of Americans at Abu Ghraib was made public.

With that possibility aside, I believe, his Byronesque romanticism blinded him to the fact that the Bush people (who were concerned with a number of matters but certainly not morality and truth) hated Saddam more than they loved the Iraqi people as I'm sure Hitchens realized when the Iraq museum was looted in front of US troops, and Rumsfeld, when asked about it, dispassionately responded, 'Stuff happens.' Did that sicken Hitchens? I don't know. What I do know is that he did not change course. Indeed 'stuff happens' and it just goes to show that even a 'clever Oxford boy' can be suckered and then become a partisan in dubious causes.

And now, when Thanatos hovers, I wonder if a whiff of doubt or regret seeps in.

Not to fear, for when Thanatos puts his arm around Christopher one last time, his famous literary friends will begin to weave tales of grand causes and passionate nights of conversation, women and good scotch, and I for one will look forward to those tales for I love a good story. However, after all of the stories have been told with the exception of one, we shall all forget that this remarkable man once composed powerful words that promoted a lie that assisted in the killing of tens of thousands of people. This is sad for I wish Hitchens well and hope one day to walk across a room, shake his hand and say, 'So, you are victorious over Thanatos, at least for a time, and I for one am glad of it.'

I like the world with Christopher Hitchens in it but I want all of Hitchens, and I hope, when words are put to paper, that his literary friends will tell it straight minus the hagiography. The man deserves nothing less.

> We dance round in a ring and suppose,
> But the Secret sits in the middle and knows.
>
> Robert Frost, 'The Secret Sits' (1942)

Journal entry

11 September 2001
Bozeman, Montana
11.39 p.m.

... today hard terrorism hit soft terrorism and, as is always the case, many innocent people have died. Some reports are now saying that thousands may have been killed but I am sure thousands have been killed.

It has taken the better part of the day for me to bridle my own anger and now I worry that Americans will overreact quickly and carelessly.

What is needed now is calm, intelligence and patience. We should focus on families that have been devastated and care for the wounded and simply attend to the immediate needs of our fellow citizens. I know a response will have to come but it must be a thoughtful and measured response, not one born of nationalistic heat. In the coming days we will have the world supporting us and offering help in ways that just a day before we could not have imagined. It is imperative that we take that goodwill and let the world surround us for a time with care and concern for that, in itself, will be one of the great blows to the terrorists. They will have moved the world closer to us and to each other and we should not squander or take that for granted.

On the other hand, if we do act carelessly we shall proceed down a road that will escalate and we will lose our way in a Muslim world that we do not understand and that lack of understanding will pull us deeper into a Middle Eastern quagmire that will, for many years I suspect, be hard to extricate ourselves from and the cost of it all will be thousands of lives – Americans and others.

We must also be very careful and vigilant about pressures coming from our own shadows that will want to accelerate the call for action. Many corporations will see this as a great opportunity for increased profits from public coffers and they will be pushing the leaders, from behind the scenes, to move forward quickly under the guise of patriotism. Many interests will now converge and I hope that the journalists will stay focused and resist falling into patriotic jingoism themselves.

What we need now is neither bravado nor swagger. We need cool, thoughtful planning and, above all, restraint. Mr. Bush has much on his shoulders. I hope that both he and the rest of us are up to the task but I don't know. I hope our leaders have read Lawrence.

> The worst sin towards our fellow creatures is
> not to hate them, but to be indifferent to
> them; that's the essence of inhumanity.
>
> George Bernard Shaw, *The Devil's Disciple* (1901)

1 December 2010

President George W. Bush
Crawford, Texas

Dear President Bush,

This is a letter I had hoped never to write but in light
of your recent public statements I feel that I now have no
choice.

On September 11, 2001 my wife, Dr. Kris Hardin, and
I watched in horror as planes flew into the 'Twin
Towers' in New York City. I spent the better part of the
day controlling my anger and realized then, that it
would be necessary, at some point, to respond to the

attacks. I supported that view, but with the caveat that first we must be very clear as to who had planned and executed the deed and felt it essential that evidence be presented to the American people prior to any military response.

I had also hoped that we, and you, would be calm and thoughtful and not act too quickly or carelessly in the midst of national shock. I was equally concerned that there would be powerful forces in the country pushing for war, for a variety of reasons and interests, under the guise of patriotism.

At the time of the attacks, and for some time thereafter, I was wishing you well and tried to understand and empathize with the pressures that you must be confronting and the multiple possibilities being weighed at such a momentous time. No matter the weight however, I was still expecting from you and my government, sober, thoughtful and lawful leadership.

As time went on, I became increasingly disturbed by your careless words such as 'Bring it on,' which I thought particularly unwise given that it would not be you in the line of fire. And then, during a journalist function, you made a joke of not finding 'weapons of mass destruction' which I found insensitive, cruel and indifferent. Sir, did you ever consider how that joke might be received by American and Iraqi families who had lost loved ones in the war?

My journal entry of 31 March 2007 expressed my concern:

> While watching the news over the last few days, I
> have seen repeated clips of the White House
> Correspondents' Dinner. There is the President
> telling jokes about subpoenas while the Speaker of the
> House laughs. I cannot tell if she is really laughing or
> being nervously polite. Then there is a clip of the
> President's main adviser and strategist, Karl Rove,
> being asked what he likes to do in his spare time. He
> answers that he likes to tear the heads off of small
> animals or some such nonsense I think. I guess that is
> humor in the Bush White House. Then a hip-hop song
> begins to play and Rove starts to dance. The MC yells,
> 'What's your name?' and Rove answers something like
> 'Master Rove.' All the while he is dancing and singing,
> a well-known television journalist is dancing behind
> him, laughing and having a grand old time. Other
> people in the audience, including a number of
> prominent news people, are laughing and moving to
> the music as well. I cannot forget that while this
> bizarre party is going on Americans and others are
> dying in Iraq and Afghanistan and it all feels so
> unseemly, so profoundly immoral (a word I rarely use)
> and insensitive. As I watched this display, I wondered
> if any of the parents who had lost children in the
> war were also watching and if so what they thought.

For even a moment did it cross their minds that their sons, daughters, fathers and mothers might have, just might have, died for nothing? I hope not.

I also wondered if when men were landing, killing and dying on Normandy, was Ike dancing the Tango somewhere safe and drinking with a bunch of scoundrels who in one way or another profited from the war. Watching the so-called journalists and power people drink, eat and dance, I realized that we are not in this together. I could not help but think of the estimates that have come out of Johns Hopkins University and the *Lancet*, which estimates that nearly 600,000 Iraqi civilians have been killed. I don't know. People, of course, dispute those numbers and I understand. If I were responsible for that much death, I would also not want it to be true.

I thought about an Iraqi mother who had lost her son and what she would be thinking as the President joked and Rove danced and the journalists laughed. Maybe she would hate us, maybe forever.

The grotesque dancing continued as I recalled the pictures of the murdered Americans in Somalia and Iraq who had had their bodies mutilated and dragged through the streets as crowds cheered and yes, danced. Rove kept moving on the screen and try as I might I could not see a difference between either savages.

At some point I began to inform myself about your tenure as Governor of Texas and discovered that, while in office, over 130 people had been executed in the state with the last being Mr. Claude Howard Jones. I found that on a number of occasions there had been media reports suggesting that you never spent more than ten to fifteen minutes reviewing capital cases. At the time, I found that reporting suspicious for surely, I thought, this could not be correct, for no one would be so cavalier with people's lives. Now I find that the DNA testing that was not done prior to Mr. Jones' execution has now been done and the result is that it is not Mr. Jones' DNA. [Reported on NPR.]

These events began to suggest a long pattern of indifference, but still, I was trying to keep an open mind and explore all alternate possibilities for such conduct. Then came Abu Ghraib, Rumsfeld's 'Stuff happens' crack, Katrina and, finally, the whiff of lies and torture.

Increasingly I became uncomfortable with you, first, as the leader of the United States, and then, with you as a man.

In London, at a dinner party, I defended you somewhat, as people questioned your intelligence. I immediately stated that I felt their criticisms were wrong-headed and that what they perceived as a lack of intelligence was really indifference. It was at that dinner party that I first voiced what I had been feeling for a number of months previously.

I am the son of a soldier who, unlike you and me, saw the hell of war first hand and who had a profound distrust of people who promoted war but seemingly were never in, or near, the fighting. This point is particularly directed to Mr. Cheney who, throughout his career, has been such a person.

I have met with such thugs before in Hungary and Turkey, Morocco and Cuba as well as in France and England. They are all of a kind and can be found in all countries. These individuals are neither left nor right but rather a type of corporate immoralist whose only allegiance is to 'more,' both for themselves and their cronies at the expense of everything and everyone else. Unlike you or Mr. Cheney I learned long ago that patriotism was more than the parroting of slogans or the wearing of a flag pin.

All of these cumulative actions started to suggest to me that perhaps you were not only an indifferent man but also a dishonorable one.

And now, I see you in an interview and you say in one breath, that you did give the OK for enhanced interrogation (torture) and then go on to say that you are content with your life and all that you have done. As a result of your statements I have had to bridle my anger again.

A courageous and honest man would not come up with 'newspeak' to disguise the reality of torture. He would call it as it is and then take responsibility for it but

I have come to understand that you are not such a man. What you are sir, as you have stated from your own mouth, is someone who gave the order to torture people in United States custody and you did that in my name and that I cannot let stand.

In Rumsfeld vs. Padilla, Justice John Paul Stevens wrote in his dissent to the court: 'For if this Nation is to remain true to the ideals symbolized by its flag, it must not wield the tools of tyrants even to resist an assault by the forces of tyranny.'

The coin of tyrants, throughout the ages, has been fear. And during your time as President you, Mr. Cheney and others, used fear to such an extent that, even today, friends whom I respect and trust say, after seeing this letter, to exercise caution and reconsider. They have said that you, and your hidden hands, could cause me misery and difficulties in addition to the serious difficulties that my dear wife and I now face. But I am not afraid of you. I am ashamed of you.

I thought it only right to contact you before writing to the International Criminal Court asking them to please begin an investigation concerning your and Mr. Cheney's admissions that you ordered torture on individuals in US custody. I know that the ICC has no jurisdiction in the United States, but I feel that it is essential for some non-American institution to involve itself in reviewing what transpired and where blame should be placed. To simply let your statements and actions pass without response makes a mockery of all that I have been taught that is fundamental to a decent and honorable society. I simply could not turn away.

Sincerely,
Michael Katakis

OTHER VOICES

(in discussion with Michael Katakis)

Your country comes across as a big bully. The expectation of Americans in my country is that they're always right. It's so damn frustrating. The American way is not always right. Should have some respect for locals.

MM, chartered accountant (male, New Zealander, 38)
Sydney airport

America is a place where you have a chance at opportunity and education. I don't like the war policy of the United States.

Rey, bartender (female, 32)
Bangkok, Thailand

I like America because it is organized and its best part is its [America's] technology.

Tan, waiter (male, 45)
Bangkok, Thailand

I don't find Americans real – they are fake. They don't have family values and think a lot about themselves. They live only for today.

DL, businessman (male, 31)
New Delhi, India (in conversation with Michael Katakis
onboard a train from Delhi to Varanasi

It [America] funds its science which is very positive.

RP, Professor of Bio-Medical engineering (female, 57)
Varanasi, India

I see negative and positive. The positive innovations and sci-entific discoveries. The negative is there is so much violence that seems to emanate from the government.

NP, computer engineer (male, 36)
Varanasi, India

I have never been to the US though have plenty of friends and relatives settled there for a long time now. I'd be happy to travel to the United States, but the idea of living there is not appealing to me anymore. There's enough crime, corruption, loneliness and growing racism to steer me away from that thought. I don't think I would like to be treated like a second-class citizen ever. Also, I'd not like to settle in the US as I don't want to lead my life driven by capital and commerce. There is more to life than reducing it to a beguiling chase after money. I don't want a surveillance state to meddle in my affairs. I don't want technology to supersede human values. I don't want to miss connecting with myself at some deep, sub-liminal level. Finally, I don't want to settle in a hypocrite state that doesn't tire of talking about democracy, freedom, justice and human rights, but violates their very foundations else-where in the world.

SQ, publicity manager (female, 32)
New Delhi, India

> The truth is that our society is populated by an unknown number of genuine monsters – people so deranged, so evil, so possessed by voices and driven by demons that no sane person can possibly ever comprehend them. They walk among us every day ... The only thing that stops a bad guy with a gun is a good guy with a gun.
>
> Wayne LaPierre, Executive Vice-President and CEO of the National Rifle Association (in a prepared response to the Newtown, Connecticut shootings, 2012)

Recently I was sitting in a London hotel ordering tea. I thanked the waitress and turned to see a woman at a nearby table staring or, more accurately, glaring at me. I smiled, nodded and went back to my tea.

'Are you American?' she asked with an accent that sounded Eastern European.

'Yes.'

She put down her paper, which carried the headline

'Massacre' about the recent shootings in Newtown, Connecticut.

'Look at this,' she said. 'It happens over and over. I don't believe in some "American Dream". Who would want such a dream, a nightmare? I sorry to disturb, but children.'

The young woman was nearly in tears and I had the feeling that she or her family had gone through something terrible, perhaps in Croatia or Serbia. I don't know. I didn't ask. I wanted to say something to her, to somehow explain that which was inexplicable, or offer something that might comfort her, and me.

'It is horrible, I know, but you see, it is just who we are and this is simply another dark American day among many. In some ways Americans are lost, I think, and have forgotten how to respect each other, to care for one another or to reason. It sometimes seems that there are those who love their rights of gun ownership more than they love America's children.

'How can that be?, you might ask, and I would say again, it is just who we are – not everyone, to be sure, but a powerful lobby comprised of a large number of Americans, powerful enough to prevent change even after such a horrible event. We have had many such events and thousands of our citizens are killed with guns every year and yet nothing changes. But it is not the guns alone, for in other societies like Canada they have guns, too, but they are not killing each other as we do in the United States. I have sometimes wondered if it is us, something about us.

'We are unconscious, I think, and because of that a danger to ourselves now, and sometimes I think that nothing can wake us from our sleepwalking, not even the murder of children. In spite of all that, I must hope. I must keep just a bit of hope alive and believe that somehow we can wake and change or it becomes too unbearable. I'm so sorry this has upset you so.'

I asked the woman if I could order her tea. She declined.

'Why so many guns, why?' she asked.

'Some people say it is our right but I think it's because we're afraid.'

'What afraid?'

'I think we Americans are afraid of each other, of everything.'

A few days later, after stepping into a cab, I heard John Lennon's voice through the speaker. 'So this is Christmas and what have you done . . .' I was silent and, while listening, the memory of another horrible day came to mind, when another American with a gun silenced that voice for ever.

Making my way to the airport, I remembered what a Frenchman had told me in the streets of Paris during a large protest:

It's funny, yes? You have all the guns in your country and still you are afraid of your government and corporations. We have no guns and the government and corporations are a little afraid of us. That's funny, yes? Don't you understand, if you don't have thousands of people in the streets, it doesn't matter. It's numbers of people standing for something that means something, not the guns.

Everywhere that I have traveled in the world, even in countries that dislike America, I have detected a quiet wish, an illusion really. It is an illusion that somewhere there is a place where all things are possible. It is a place not unlike Oz, where you can get anything: a brain, a heart or a future. When the detective in *The Maltese Falcon* asks Sam Spade, 'What is it?' while holding the predator statuette, Humphrey Bogart tells him that it is the stuff that dreams are made of. His line has manifested itself in the imaginations of millions of people as a country, and that country is America or, more to the point, the fictional narrative of America that we Americans have been selling for some time now.

I have learned that few things can anger people more than to have their hopes, which are wrapped up in their illusions, proven false. That is why people around the world can be conflicted, and love and hate America at the same time. America has become a repository of sorts for the hopes, unrealized dreams and wishes of millions. It matters not that the illusion is not true, for myth and belief are powerful forces in the human imagination, and I had a sense that the woman at the hotel was not only angry about the tragedy itself but also disappointed that we had not been what she had dreamed us to be.

I feel for such people, very much so, for they often have difficult lives or have been through something tragic and very much need a life preserver in the form of a perfect place to hang their dreams on. As an American I also long for such a place.

For a number of years now we Americans have lived in a world of black and white and increasingly seem unable to evolve or even consider that we may be wrong, even slightly, in our views about ourselves, or be open to how the rest of the western world perceives us. We have consistently behaved as if we have nothing to learn from anyone, even each other. It has often felt to me that, contained within our hubris and ignorance, Americans have come to believe that we have reached some kind of evolutionary societal perfection. How very odd indeed.

George W. Bush was not unique when he said, 'You are with us or with the terrorists,' as he challenged the world to get with us or else. It would seem that winning the argument has become more important than realizing viable solutions to our very serious problems, even the mass murder of children and the role of guns and the National Rifle Association (NRA) in our society. If the killing of children cannot elicit the realization that perhaps, at a minimum, a change in thinking should at least be considered, then I simply do not know what will bring us to a point of national catharsis.

Over and over again, following such tragedies, the NRA and gun activists have taken their old and tattered talking points out of storage and, without reflection or real ideas, simply repeated what a majority of Americans have heard before. It is all so automatic and it has worked in obstructing any meaningful changes to gun control in the United States. It is tragic. In America it is nearly impossible to have a nuanced discussion about guns because, in the view of many gun activists, any attempt to moderate the manufacture or sale of any weapon is viewed as a threat to the access to all weapons. It is a paranoid's world view.

Whether we Americans face it or not, the reality is that the world is not black and white: it is shades of gray, and a thinking society is best served when it is poised and unafraid to adjust when a change of course becomes self-evidently necessary to the well-being of the entire nation, not just that of a vocal and well-funded minority.

I grew up with guns and I remember the NRA when it seemed rather innocent, a local organization comprised of friends and neighbors who taught gun safety and the proper care of a weapon as well as a gun owner's responsibilities. But the NRA of today is nothing like that at all. It is a corporate, extremist lobbying organization that is incapable of holding any balanced views. Their business is not to be balanced. Their business is to represent gun manufacturers. The NRA today is nothing more than a very powerful lobbyist for the gun manufacturers.

The irony is that if guns are banned in this country one day, a major player that will have made that possible is the NRA itself. The NRA's long-held extremist positions, like once making a case for the public's right to purchase Teflon bullets that go through bulletproof vests, which have been referred to by some criminal elements as 'cop killers', not to mention their support for the continued sale of assault rifles and high-capacity ammunition magazines, have many citizens, including some gun owners, viewing the NRA and its supporters as something either out of touch or abhorrent.

I believe them to be the latter, because time and time again, following the killings, the NRA has come out with the mantra that what is needed to protect everyone from such monsters in the future is not gun control but more guns in the hands of 'law-abiding' citizens, with the additional perk of being able to carry them as well. This all-purpose NRA mantra, beyond being insensitive when coming on the heels of such killings, is also factually incorrect. There were armed guards at both Columbine and at Virginia Tech, and Fort Hood was a military base for goodness sake.

Law-enforcement officers have illustrated their concerns to me as follows: if they rushed into a movie theater where a shooting was in progress only to be confronted by multiple persons with guns drawn, even with all of their training, how would they know who to shoot? Who is the bad guy and how does the officer make a determination in fractions of seconds? If a law-enforcement officer, with all of his or her training, is so concerned, then how does this play out with all the armed 'good citizens', who presumably have much less training, if any?

The NRA never answers such questions, nor do they seemingly listen to law enforcement or anyone else. Forget about rights or laws: they are, first and foremost, about helping their clients, the gun manufacturers, and they do so by strenuously lobbying our frightened, cash-strapped representatives to water down legislation that would restrict gun rights and their manufacture. This must change.

As surely as a tide ebbs and flows, shootings like the recent ones in Newtown create momentary drama in America. The police on TV tell the same stories about what needs to be done, as do the media's talking heads, who offer a grotesque form of entertainment following such events. Politicians compose legislation to add restrictions, and that legislation is pared down or dropped altogether due to the NRA's powerful lobbying muscle. The newspapers' headlines ask the questions they have asked before and that have gone unanswered and go unanswered still. And then, after all of the commotion, indignation and tears recede, we get on with our lives until the next tragedy.

This would suggest that all is peaceful between those dramatic multiple killings, but that is not true. Every day our fellow citizens, children and women among them, are being murdered and maimed with guns. In fact, they are killed by the thousands every year. More people are killed by guns each year than died on September 11.

Sadly, I have come to realize that 'those' people are the 'invisible murdered' among us. They are not invisible to their community or their loved ones, but to the nation as a whole. The story is not big enough. It is the large multiple murders, like a blockbuster film, that attract a national audience these days and after the reporters and commentators and politicians pack up their curiosity and indignation they move on, as most of us do. And yet, every day throughout America the body count increases. Those invisible among us are children and women and seniors and teenagers. They are our fellow citizens and they are all 'our' children.

We Americans should not fear changing course and asking questions and demanding that we and our leaders consider the well-being of the nation above the wishes of businessmen and zealots whose first priorities are to themselves. The sad fact is that in America, until it happens to someone we know personally, little if anything wakes us from our indifference. Americans have become desensitized to violence. This is clear from the countless times violence has happened in our schools, not to mention on the streets and in the homes of America over and over again.

With all the hand-wringing, protests and proposed legislation, as well as the newspaper and TV coverage, I suspect, though I hope to be proven wrong, that little will change, even after the mass murder of children, and that is simply unacceptable, for we owe a debt to one another, and that debt demands that we reflect on our positions but also fight for public policy and legislation that is reasoned and sensible and successful in regard to the well-being of each other and the most vulnerable among us.

My plane touched down in San Francisco and after renting a car I made myself comfortable for the two-hour drive south to Carmel. I played with the car's radio, moving from station to station, and then John Lennon's voice filled the cabin. 'Oh, come on, now,' I thought. 'Are you kidding me?' For it seemed that Lennon had followed me across the sea, as if to remind me of the place to which I had returned and the wish I should keep striving for, before falling into my own complacency. I drove down the crowded freeway in the dark as he sang.

So this is Christmas
And what have you done
Another year over
And a new one just begun ...

A very merry Christmas
And a happy New Year
Let's hope it's a good one
Without any fear

Amen.

11 AN ABSENCE OF POETRY

> To live is the rarest thing in the world. Most
> people exist, that is all.
>
> Oscar Wilde, *The Soul of Man under Socialism* (1891)

I have heard a lovely sentiment in Paris, *L'esprit de l'escalier*, and there are many definitions as to what it means.

The definition that I have taken as my own was told to me by an elderly barman in the 16th arrondissement. For him, the 'spirit of the staircase' is the image of a man who follows a woman up the stairs. She is known or unknown, young or old, and when he catches a glimpse of her ankle it fires his imagination, suggesting what might have been or could be. He went on to say that such feelings, like the anticipation of romance, are even sweeter than the actual event because the dreams of what could be take us far beyond what was, even the fact that youth is no longer ours. His description was a poem of longing and hope. It was about youth and age, love and loss, and I was deeply touched by the conviction in his voice and the emotion in his eyes.

The bartender was a man of about seventy and I remember how beautifully he spoke and how he was swept away by his own words. I suspect that his heart still desired, as all hearts do, and at times his own dreams of what could have been gave him pleasure, with the taste of something bittersweet. Even with time no longer on his side the lovely barman in his starched white coat was dancing the dance of life and did so beautifully. With each word and step he seemed transformed into what must have been his once-younger self. He made me smile and I was so happy to be in his presence as he danced and recited his poetry of living.

There is an absence of poetry in the United States and that is not at all surprising, for we Americans are a people of lists, not poetry. That is a choice of course and we have chosen unwisely. Ours is a practicality so stifling now that it removes much of the subtlety and sweetness from our lives. The consequences of such choices, in my opinion, are the most efficient assassins of serendipity and self-reflection in the western world. Apart from being very dangerous, it is much less fun to be shackled to a practicality so severe that often there is little room left for serendipity to inform or surprise.

When I lived in Paris, it always seemed that I was being treated to a series of daily surprises, for the French, in some way, seem to inhabit and embrace the simple pleasures of life. To watch them when it is strawberry season, for instance, is to delight again in a pleasure that I had once known as a child, but in adulthood had forgotten. It is easy to forget such simple, lovely things in America, for we don't dance, and the lists we compose and steer our lives by are often nothing more than banal and trivial reminders of more and more trivial tasks to be done. How very sad indeed.

In fact, our obsession with our devices now allows us to make even more lists, and these devices are with us at all times, and they do not, as many insist, connect us to the world as much as distance us from it. We move from screen to screen, rarely seeing life take place in the spaces between. Escalating convenience has been a very profitable lie but with a very high cost. Increasingly, we are leaving little room in our lives for chance itself to sweep us off our feet. Step by step we are stripping away the small, beautiful things, replacing them not with each other but with illusions of control and efficiency, while in actuality we are simply becoming more frazzled, with a constant and nagging feeling that something has been left undone. Something has. We have forgotten to dance.

In this kind of environment, rationalizations and self-delusions find rich soil in which to grow. There are the rationalizations that one needs so much to survive or that we Americans work hard and are on the go because of our work ethic or, as a result of all the running around, we have achieved the status of being the most productive country on earth. It is not true, but truth is just one casualty in a land without poetry. We take ourselves much too seriously and that attitude actually contributes to our illusions of superiority. Those illusions have exacted a terrible price for ourselves, and for others in places with names like Iraq and Afghanistan, Chile and Vietnam. We Americans, like empires before us, have often confused assumptions and hubris with knowledge and wisdom.

A dear friend in London once said something so simple and profound that I nearly dismissed it. He said that he thought it very good that England was now well past its colonial superiority around the world and that the British were now able to exhale. They had made it through that period and now could get on with other things that were good and generous and more fun, more fulfilling. I loved his comments, for they seemed to me a template of sorts, one that we Americans might use some day.

I know that all of this talk about the poetry of living can seem rather a quaint and esoteric idea, but it does have weight, for there is a consequence when an individual or society have an absence of poetry in their daily lives. The absence of poetry begins to render us blind to the world's smaller, detailed brush strokes, forcing us to concentrate on the large sweeping ones, but they do not reveal where the gold is hidden. In fact, the gold is not hidden at all. It resides in the lovely stories that compose themselves in front of us every day. It is the little girl in a summer dress wearing the strange 1950s sunglasses running past, or the older couple on a park bench holding hands. It is the taste of gelato on a hot summer's day and the conversation of friends around a table. It is a million small, beautiful things and it is from that poetry that we get our virtues of kindness and empathy, generosity and joy, as well as the self-reflection that helps us to evaluate what we are doing and why.

The poetry of living has a way of putting in perspective those things that would rob us of our lives and helps us to engage and enjoy the world around us. Simply put, the poetry keeps us in the world and reminds us that we are connected, just as John Donne wrote. Perhaps the poetry itself is 'the main'. Americans today have less and less of a sense of this and as a result I have seen us grow more distant from one another and more alone. It does not have to be this way. When we Americans are thinking clearly, we can be a pretty good bunch, but for a long time now we seem to have forgotten how to get along, how to modify our beliefs or how to be silent for a time and just reflect.

Antoine de Saint-Exupéry once suggested that what he was afraid of was the 'tyranny of petty things' and he had cause to be afraid, for all those petty things that we ourselves embrace, silently and relentlessly, day in and day out, rob from us the only things of value that we shall ever possess: time and our humanity.

The dance, of course, is a metaphor for letting life in. For being more thoughtful and kind, more generous and, finally, free of implacable ideologies that close the mind and harden the heart. It is so much more fun to be engaged in the world rather than to constantly be afraid of it. Are there dangers? Of course there are, but the greatest danger is sitting out the dance and coming to the end of one's life only to discover that the finite and precious time has been spent in denial or in fear.

I for one wish my fellow Americans the dance. I will hold

out my hand and then, like the wonderful old barman in Paris, perhaps we will dance the dance of our time together. While walking up the staircase we can dream of what might have been and what still could be.

12 THE LAST NIGHT TRAIN: WHAT IS A COUNTRY FOR?

> We have lingered in the chambers of the sea
> By sea-girls wreathed with seaweed red and brown
> Till human voices wake us, and we drown.
>
> T.S. Eliot, *from* 'The Love Song of
> J. Alfred Prufrock' (1920)

As of late I have wondered if redemption has a shelf life. Is there some kind of use-by date or line that, once crossed, makes nearly impossible the ability to correct our course? I don't know, but it seems one must engage in a great deal of denial in order to stay on a track which, when looked at closely, runs counter to what that society proclaims as its values. At some point one would think a choice could be made between the illusion of self-righteousness and the real thing. Perhaps not.

My late father, a former soldier, once told me that words like honor, duty and courage are just that: words that lie on the floor until our actions give them life. He believed it is in actions of sacrifice, not for grand manufactured causes but in the little actions of day-to-day living, that such virtues are to be found. It sounds so simple, doesn't it, but I have been thinking, what if it really is just that simple.

What is a country for? Is it simply to be an arm of business, advocating and then creating laws and regulations that serve the interests of a select few, often at the expense of the common good? Does it exist to exercise power over weaker nations, forcing them, by coercion or other unsavory means, to do that which conflicts with the country's own interests? If so, to what end?

Should a nation allow business a free rein even when its actions reduce citizens to a cash crop annually harvested for the benefit of the corporation's interests? Should a country invest in education and roads and infrastructure before it spends the 'people's' money on ever more military hardware, or should a nation be something more than that, something that rises, or attempts to rise, above commerce alone, striving to better all of the country's citizens?

Should a country be first and foremost humane and less a grouping of economic tribes that finally devolve into nothing more than a giant store? If not, then who among us would want our children to die for such a thing? Who then would believe the lofty words that would precede a call to arms? Would there still be the cheering crowds and if so which flags would they wave: the stars and stripes or a variety of flags with corporate logos?

Clearly a country can be an economically viable state while at the same time an unsuccessful nation, for to be a country is not to be one thing or the other but rather to be many things, with the priority being the real interests and well-being of all of its people. The rich don't need much help: they're doing just fine.

The United States today very much reminds me of another place in a time not so long ago. In England, the East India Company, along with the government and monarchy, morphed into a kind of corporation with each of its branches helping to facilitate the other's wishes and goals. They profited well from dark agreements and did despicable things, using lofty words to sell a perverse and not so cloaked suggestion of racial superiority and nationalism. They used biblical phrases to justify their actions and to declare their mission of wishing to 'help' the godless people find God, before relieving the newly faithful of their country's treasures.

The British used the same words that we Americans use today when invading other countries. We declare it is to 'help' the people, but it is odd that more often than not the people we always try to help sit on oil or diamonds, minerals or geography that help facilitate or stabilize our own business interests. Is that what a country is for?

I look forward to the day when we use our own escape hatch and let the empire that even now is crumbling around us finally fall. It is my hope that as a result of that we shall be able to finally exhale and, for the first time in a long time, look around and see each other and the world and our place in it in a different and more humane way. Quite simply, I think our best days lie in front of us, after empire, when we may be able to remake ourselves into not merely a powerful country, but a meaningful one, that places virtue, truth and ethics at a level higher than monetary profit. As Ernest Hemingway once wrote, 'Wouldn't it be nice to think so?'

MY FINAL OPENING FAREWELL

> Come! Let us make that bargain. Think of
> me at my best, if circumstances should ever
> part us!
>
> Charles Dickens, *David Copperfield*, 1850

It was death that brought us back to America.

Kris' and my life in Rapallo and Paris was a simple and beautiful one and saying that now reminds me of how some Americans responded when they heard how we lived and where. There was often that first tinge of jealousy, followed by the assumption that we were 'rich people' who could not understand what 'working people', with their many obligations, go through. 'It must be nice to be rich and travel the world,' one woman told us with a spoonful of resentment, while another, with her Calvinist disapproval, said, 'Well, I'd love to do that but I take my responsibilities seriously.' I'm still trying to understand that one.

Kris and I were not rich in terms of money, but we understood what so many Americans did not, which is that one does not need to be rich to live a good life. What is needed is imagination, courage and a poet's heart at taking risks to make it so. Money is always helpful, but not a guarantee. Money does not do. It is heart and desire that finally takes the step.

We initially left the United States in protest because of the increasingly aggressive behavior of President Bush and others following September 11 and because of the American people themselves, who seemed unable to speak about anything except money, business or 'getting' the people 'we' perceived were against 'us'. It felt that life in the United States, the poetry of life, was dying and we hungered to live by a rhythm that we had come to know when living in other countries. We wanted out of the consumer corporate state that seemed to have a never-ending line of salesmen who called you at home, offering things or threatening things or asking you to get on this or that website to do one task or another.

The nation of menial tasks and lists was unacceptable to us and we were not going to allow it to rob us of our lives or drown us in a trivial sea. We wanted a simple life filled with daily work done well and time together that was not interrupted other than by the people we loved. We wanted to get far away from what we came to refer to as the American Noise.

Kris left first. She traveled to Italy hoping to find an apartment that we could afford and work well in. In Rapallo she found a small one with a remarkably large veranda that overlooked a gulley filled with lemon and olive trees and, to the left, views of the Ligurian Sea. She telephoned after sending photographs.

'Michael, the apartment is very small and simple, but the veranda will be a wonderful place for you and me to write and work and to take our meals. It's only a short walk to the sea and the afternoon vegetable market is only about one and a half miles away. What do you think?'

'It sounds lovely, but can we afford it?'

'Well, I've worked it out. The apartment is six hundred euros a month. The lunches you and I would prepare after going to the vegetable market and pasta shop would run to about six or seven euros a day, and for dinner I found a wonderful bar on the water that serves Prosecco and when you order before 6 p.m. they give you lots of little plates of ham and cheese, olives and vegetables. It costs seven euros for the two of us. So I think that we can live very well for about fourteen hundred euros a month. What do you think?"

'I think you're a genius.'

And so I left the United States and landed in Milan and from there I traveled by train to Genova and on to Rapallo. Arriving at the station, my beautiful, sun-drenched wife was waiting with open arms, a big kiss and a small bottle of Limoncello, which she dipped her finger into and then put to my lips.

'Welcome to Italy, my love. Welcome home.'

And it was home. Our days began the same way. We would sit on our veranda at first light and have our fruit and yogurt with coffee or tea and then we would set to work. I would begin to write while my beautiful new neighbor across the gulley swept her veranda topless. After a month she would wave and say 'Ciao' as the scent of lemon from the trees below was carried on the wind.

After a good morning's work, Kris and I, with net bags in hand, would walk to the vegetable market. The stall we most frequented was owned by a stunningly beautiful, buxom woman who, unbelievably, was seventy years old.

After seeing me there for over a month, she began to beautifully and wickedly tease me by bending over her produce, which gave a view of her ample breasts.

'Ciao, Myco. *Meloni?*' she would say as I turned red and looked somewhere, anywhere, other than at her and her breasts. This of course pleased her and caused her to laugh and tease even more.

'*Un melone o due?*' she asked, while leaning over the vegetables. I would start to laugh and she touched my hand, smiling provocatively, and she did so shamelessly in front of Kris, which gave Kris great pleasure, especially when the woman asked, 'Why are you with such a skinny woman? Yes, I know she is very beautiful, but older woman, Myco, oh yes, older woman.'

Kris and I realized that our lovely, playful market lady was the real poetry of living and one of the threads being woven into our lives, making us part of the tapestry that was all around us. We cherished that world and never took for granted the lives we were living.

After lunch we would rest and then go for a swim before returning to review the day's work, checking it again and preparing it for the following morning. The evenings were magical and sometimes, instead of dinner, we would catch a bus past Santa Margarita to a place we had found that always seemed to us an undiscovered oasis. Once, late at night, Kris and I, with a bottle of grappa, laid on the small beach naked and then swam in the dark and warm water as the reflected stars danced around us. It was a beautiful moment and it could not last.

The next day began like the others. We were deep into our work and the work was going well. I had heard from a publisher interested in my book and that interest had me working harder so as to complete it by the fall. It was a day filled with pleasure and promise and a routine that Kris and I had come to love. That evening we were going to dinner at the home of Giuseppe and Betty Gargano.

Giuseppe and Betty owned the best provisions shop in Rapallo and we had become friends. Through Giuseppe we had learned about dried beans, olives and cheese and the different Parma hams. He had taught us how to make the best minestrone soup I have ever had and he introduced me to some of the old fishermen still working the sea.

That night was one of those evenings that never leaves the heart or mind. There we were, struggling with each other's languages and yet communicating perfectly. The laughter and wine flowed and never was there a hint that this evening would be our last together.

We returned to our apartment and were still laughing when the phone rang. It was Kris' mother and she was in a panic. Kris' father had just dropped dead and could not be resuscitated. I held my dear wife as she cried and then cried myself, not just for Kris or her father and mother, but for our perfect life that I somehow knew was over. We stepped on to the veranda and looked up at the sky filled with stars. We stood there for a long time and were still there when the sun came up.

Kris took a long last look at the sea and the olive and lemon trees and then waved one last time to our lovely, wacky neighbor who, topless, was sweeping away. Within a few hours she was en route to California. I stayed behind to close the apartment that we would never see again and within a few days I was driving to Paris with our belongings and our dog and cat, Angus and Thelma.

In San Francisco, Kris was there to meet me and she could see I was sick and tired and, while happy to see her, heartbroken to be in the land of lists once again. She, too, was heartbroken, but reminded me that we would only be there for six or seven months to help her mother and then we would return to our beautiful, simple life. We never did.

Some months later, after doing what we could for her mother, we began to make plans for our return. One morning, something so small happened that even now it seems like a faraway dream. Kris woke with a headache and that headache was coming from a brain tumor.

For the time that remained, our lives were punctuated by fear and much of that fear came not only from the tumor but also from the constant barrage of demands placed upon us from the business people of medicine in the United States.

There were no lovely market ladies with kind, sweet and provocative teasing; there was no poetry, and it broke our hearts.

Between Kris' treatments we were able to spend two good years going back and forth to Paris and Italy but it was not the same, knowing that we always had to return to the land of lists, but still, we tried to be positive in spite of everything that was put in our way.

On Kris' last day she asked me to read to her as we had always done for each other.

'What would you like me to read?' I asked.

'Do you remember that watercolor that I painted for you? The one of the Venice doorway?'

'Of course I remember. I love that watercolor.'

'Do you remember the quote from *Invisible Cities* that I included with it?'

'Of course, my love. It's right here. The framed painting and the quote. You know, I've told you so many times, it's my most cherished possession.'

'Read it to me.'

I picked up the double frame, looking again at the beautiful watercolor, and read Italo Calvino's passage from *Invisible Cities*:

Arriving at each new city the traveller finds again a past of his that he did not know he had: the foreignness of what you no longer are or no longer possess lies in wait for you in foreign, unpossessed places.

'That's so beautiful. It's the story of our lives, isn't it?' she asked.

'Oh yes, my love, that and so much more.'

Within a few hours the nurse came in to tell me that I had to tell Kris that it was all right to go.

'But it's not all right,' I said.

'You must.'

I never could say it was all right, but what I did say was, 'My love, your bags are packed and on the train. You catch this one and make a place for us ahead like you did in Italy. I'll catch the next. I love you.' A short time later she was on her way.

There are many good and decent people in the United States, but I have come to know that most Americans are sleepwalking. They bypass the misery around them and repeat to themselves and others the same banal and insincere rationalizations meant not to inform, but rather excuse and dismiss. A number of my fellow Americans worked at their jobs and robbed me of the precious little time I had left with my wife, and I don't know how to forgive them for that. The poetry in my life was Kris, but poets mean nothing in the land of lists and that makes for a lonely and dead place.

I must leave the United States again now, and alone and for the last time, not because of Bush or the war or the medical system or Republicans, but because of the lack of kindness here and the way we treat one another. I will not accept that kind of life and I will not live among people who choose to be blind and unconscious.

The train is coming for me, as it is for us all, and when it arrives, I wish to be in a place where people are laughing and loving and smelling lemon on the wind. I would like to think that the big buxom market lady would again hold my hand and smile just before I board and then whisper, 'That skinny beautiful girl you love is waiting for you at the station just a little down the track.'

In such a place, with such people, I will think of Kris and poetry but not of lists. I will be grateful for the life I have had and in the hour before I depart, though not a man of faith, I shall say a prayer, not for myself but for my countrymen and women. I will wish for them the smell of lemon and poetry and a simple and beautiful life in a place where people care for one another more than they care for lists. It will be their choice, as it always has been, and I will pray that they choose wisely and with their hearts.

THE DARK FOUNTAIN OF WISHES' ENDS

(for Mary Katharine Lewis)

At the Dark Fountain I held the
Coin chancing a wish until you
Loved me away from the water's
Whisper of promised peace

Again and again the broken
Words from my selfish storms
Rained upon you but you
Sought no shelter, instead
Tracking me down Sorrow's
Canyons your request echoing
From their walls, stay, stay

The jagged words cut through
The air answering your call,
Striking the heart and as your
Silence lay bleeding you held

Out a hand, a reminder that
My life was not lived for myself
Alone

In a Paris café I placed the
Coins into your hand and you
Wished me shipwrecked on the
Island of Memory where once the
World was young and everything
Seemed for ever

From across the world I
Return to your fountain, my
Pockets filled with the wishes
I carry for you, my
Defiant Beautiful Friend

ACKNOWLEDGMENTS

Not so long ago I had the great pleasure to make the acquaintance of Mr. Ian Chapman. Initially we met by phone and discussed work that needed both of our attention. After concluding our business we talked of the world and of literature and many other things.

What I remember most is how easily the conversation flowed and how much laughter was exchanged on the overseas line, almost as if we had known each other for years. At one point Ian told me how much he liked my last book and asked if I was working on anything presently. After explaining a book of essays, he asked if he could read one. I forwarded two and, in what seemed like less than a day, I heard back from an enthusiastic Ian, telling me how much he liked the work and that he would like to read more. From that day Ian, head of Simon & Schuster UK, has championed my work and me and I am profoundly grateful.

Ian's enthusiasm was passed on to his colleague Ms. Lou Johnson, head of Simon & Schuster Australia, and after my arrival in Australia for other publishing matters, it was Ms. Johnson who championed the work and extended such warm and kind hospitality that even now when I think of her and her husband Douglas and her two daughters Ella and Ruby who have the 'special words' it brings a smile to my face. Ms. Johnson and her remarkable colleagues in Australia as well as Ian's in London have left me dazed, and wondering how I got so lucky.

I also wish to thank Ms. Suzanne Baboneau, Simon & Schuster UK, for her gracious hospitality, kind words and enthusiasm for my work. In a changing world where professionalism is often just a word, Mr. Chapman, Ms. Johnson and Ms. Baboneau have reminded me what a publisher looks and sounds like and what they do. As I have said, I am lucky not only to have been embraced by such professionals but also to be able to call them my friends.

My luck has continued by having Ms. Jessica Leeke as my editor. At first I was taken aback by someone who looked nineteen years of age, wondering how she could possibly understand the things I was writing about, but quickly came to realize after a few of her suggestions that I was talking and working with a very talented individual who cared deeply for my words and exercised great care in their editing. Unbelievably, my editor in Australia, Ms. Roberta Ivers, was another person who cared deeply about what I was writing and took great care, with her extensive expertise, to help my book be the best it could be, for which I am very grateful.

I also want to thank Mr. Rahul Srivastava, head of Simon

& Schuster in India, and his staff, for their courtesy and hospitality.

I wish to thank the wonderful poet and publisher at Gallimard, Mr. Louis Chevallier, for championing my work in France. Thanks to Col. Graham Cundy, Royal Marines, Special Forces, and to everyone at the British Library, in particular Ms. Carole Holden, Mr. John Falconer and Ms. Sarah Frankland, who weathered many of 'our' storms yet still managed to care for our work in a way that made Kris and I very happy. To Michel and Dominique who always had fresh flowers on the bar in Paris and to Serge and Gerrard Tafane at the Rotonde.

Quite simply, I would not be here today if not for the following people and try as I might I shall never be able to thank them properly. The dark days of Kris' illness even now are hard for me to comprehend, for the horror of what took place over a number of years did finally break me and it was only because of the following people that I managed to survive. This is in no way overstatement, merely a statement of fact.

To Lynn Badertscher, who was Kris' old dear friend and then became mine and was always there, and Tanya Johnson and Wendy Ellis-Smith. I simply have no words. Thank you to Jean O'Brien and Elizabeth Schneider, Donna Nico and Beverla Miles. To the kind and gentle Alan Lewis and to Kati Lewis, who wrote me nearly every week during Kris' extended illness, saving me from madness. Thank you for being there on Kris' last day, Kati. Thanks to DeWitt Sage.

To Michael Palin, who has been so much more than a good

and dear friend to Kris and I for many years and who, with his dear wife Helen, always made a place for us at their table. To Brian Spence who, after learning Kris was near the end, flew from Paris to be with her and me. To Peter Luff, who stayed close. To Dr. Peter English, who loved Kris and would never take a dime for her dental work nor for that matter mine. To Jerry Fielder, who would not allow me to face Kris' last night alone, and to Daniel Campbell. To Ms. Barbara Stone, who always had tea waiting, Randell Bishop for his friendship and scones and to Hal Gurnee. To my dear friend Cary Porter, who has always been there. To Peggy Gotthold and Lawrence Van Velzer, Steve and Nancy Hauk, Enzo Pagano, and the 'London gang', who are Michael and Sarmi Lawrence, Denise Prior, Cherry Cole, Richard Fawkes, Julian Davies and Clare Gibson. To Dennis High and Jim and Gloria Dougherty. Much love and thanks to Patrick and Carol Hemingway, Don High, Eleanor Hardin and Douglas Hardin. To Jeff Wilson, Susan Moldow and others at Simon and Schuster US. To Don and Mary Wurtz and to Mary and Gerard Fort.

I would like to thank the people at Wilton's in London, who have always made me feel welcome and were so very kind in helping Kris when she could no longer walk. It was a lovely afternoon and our last together in London. Finally, to Ms. Melissa Sullivan, who was kind and showed me that deep within the depths of another sea I could breathe.

(ONE LAST TIME) MY TRUE NORTH

Journal entry

29 September 2003
Sounio, Greece

Kris and I have hiked up to the ruins of the Temple of
Poseidon and the sea opens up before us. The
breathtaking vista makes clear why the temple was built
here. If Poseidon, the god of the sea, had lived anywhere
he would have lived here. It is magnificent and we are
gloriously alone with these ruins created some 440 years
before Christ.

Kris is sitting on one of the massive overturned
columns as she opens her rucksack and pulls out the
small watercolor box I bought for her in Paris years
before. She is turned sideways and with her large
sunbonnet and skirt, in silhouette, she looks like a
traveller from another century in one of those old books
that you would find in London.

From the day I met her, I thought her the most beautiful woman I had ever seen. As a young anthropologist she had just returned from living in West Africa for some years.

Brains and beauty I had thought at our first meeting when I could not find the words, any words. She was kind as I stumbled. She has always been kind.

As I watched her painting, I could not help but think of all of the miles we had traveled together since that first meeting, thousands of miles. I have learned much from her for she is always engaged in the world, wanting to understand that which she does not understand. She is my center, my friend and my True North, always guiding and welcoming me home.

ABOUT THE AUTHOR

Michael Katakis is the author of a number of books, including *Despatches* (limited special edition), *The Vietnam Veterans Memorial, Ernest Hemingway: Artifacts from a Life, Traveller: Observations from an American in Exile* and *Photographs & Words* (with Kris L. Hardin). He is the editor of *Sacred Trusts: Essays on Stewardship and Responsibility* and *Excavating Voices: Listening to Photographs of Native Americans.*

His work has been translated into multiple languages and his writing and photography have been collected by a wide range of institutions, including the National Portrait Gallery in Washington, D.C.; the Victoria and Albert Museum and the British Library in London; and Stanford University's Special Collections Department. In 1999, Michael was elected Fellow of the Royal Geographical Society. He lives in Paris and Carmel.